Straight From The Heart

Hannah Rose

authorHOUSE®

AuthorHouse™
1663 Liberty Drive
Bloomington, IN 47403
www.authorhouse.com
Phone: 1-800-839-8640

Published by AuthorHouse 4/9/2013

ISBN: 978-1-4817-3695-4 (sc)
ISBN: 978-1-4817-3696-1 (e)

This book is printed on acid-free paper.

Unless otherwise indicated, all scripture quotes are from the Spirit Filled Life Bible,
New King James Version, copyright © 1991 by Thomas Nelson, Inc.

Scripture verses cited from the King James Version are taken from The King James
Compact Reference Bible, Red Letter, © 2000 by Zondervan

Commentary references taken from Matthew Henry's Commentary on the Whole
Bible, complete and unabridged. Copyright 1991 by Hendrickson Publishers, Inc.

References to words cited from Strong's with a numerical attachment are quoted
from The New Strong's Exhaustive Concordance of the Bible. James Strong, LL.D.,
S.T.D. Copyright 1995 Thomas Nelson Publishers

Table of Contents

"For you see your calling, brethren,
That not many wise according to the flesh,
Not many mighty, not many noble, are called.
But God has chosen the foolish things of the
World to put to shame the wise, and God has
chosen the weak Things of the world
To put to shame the things which are mighty;
And the base things of the world
And the things which are despised
God has chosen, and the things which are not,
To bring to nothing the things that are,
That no flesh should glory in His presence."

I Corinthians 1:26-29

Prelude

This is a compilation of thoughts and entries that can in and of themselves stand-alone as a daily devotional for a month, be read in succession, or read as the Holy Spirit moves you. The common thread that holds them together is Christ and His sovereignty. His Word provides us with everything we need for comfort, wisdom, sound advice, direction, and commandments.

At this juncture of my life I think I have completed my education. My degree is not in biblical studies, although I don't think that it is what is important to the writing of this book. There may be mistakes or errors (although I hope not), but please know that it is written in humility trying to express God's love for our hurting times, encouragement, and lessons that I have gleaned through my own experiences.

I have written about how God has gotten me through the tough times and the words that He has spoken to my heart through times of difficulty and trial. My hope is that you will find what I have shared helpful for your own journey.

I owe a debt of gratitude to my children, because without them I may have continued to walk on a path without regard for God's providence and grace, and for their helping me to let God work His perfect patience in me until such a time in which I see the fulfillment of His Word in our lives.

Origin

"Losing love is like a window in your heart.
Everybody sees you're blown apart.
Everybody sees the wind blow."
Paul Simon "Graceland"

Everyone can relate to heartache. There's not a person on earth who can't relate to heart pain. You don't get a pass in this life. No one is exempt.

If you are a follower of Jesus Christ, sometimes it seems that you experience more than your share of the worst and the most excruciating pain that you have ever felt. Some days it may feel like more than you can bear.

Then there's grace.

God's Word is very clear in telling us that if we walk with Him according to His will, He will never give us more that we can bear and He will never leave us. Deuteronomy 31:6 tells us:

> *"Be strong and of good courage, do not fear nor be afraid of them; for the LORD your God, He is the One who goes with you. He will not leave you nor forsake you."*

And again in verse 8: *"And the LORD, He is the One*

> *who goes before you. He will be with you; He will not leave*
> *you nor forsake you; do not fear nor be dismayed."*

This book is born from a heart that has had to lean on Jesus so strongly most days that you really could not have been able to tell where I ended and He began. That's just what He intended. He wants us to trust Him like our life depended upon it. And it does.

This is not just another devotional. It's a collection of micro-stories about life. Maybe you've experienced similar circumstances and can relate to some of the themes. Read it as the Lord prompts you, and my prayer is that when you read it, the timeliness of the message would be perfect for your moment in life.

That's just how God works, mysterious only in the fact that we don't understand God's methodology - what He uses as a cool drink of water for a parched soul. Each person and circumstance is unique.

He knows what you need, lonely, hurting, and frightened, sojourner, and He will supply it. For His word says:

> *"And my God shall supply all your need according to His*
> *riches and glory by Christ Jesus." Philippians 4:19*

May you be richly provided for this day with everything that you need, and the ability to be content with whatever God supplies.

Sustaining Word

It's funny to me that as I began to conceptualize the writing of this devotional the words to Graceland popped into my head. (This will take on greater meaning later in the book).

Mr. Simon hit the nail on the head when he sang that losing love is like the window of your heart. Everyone can see it's torn apart. That's what it feels like sometimes, doesn't it? That one more ounce of hurt is just going to make your heart crack right open and everyone will be able to tell.

And you may think for certain that people will be judging you for that (you fill in the blank) - break up, divorce, job loss, custody issues, financial crisis...

Navigating through painful circumstances leaves us vulnerable, undressed, like we are unable to cover the reproach bearing down on us.

Well, God nailed that hurt of yours to the cross of Christ. Colossians 2:14 tells us:

> *"Having wiped out the handwriting of requirements that was against us, which was contrary to us. And He has taken it out of the way, having nailed it to the cross."*

The KJV version says: *"Blotting out the handwriting of ordinances that was against us, which was contrary to us, and took it out of the way, nailing it to his cross."*

Blotting out is referenced to Strong's #1813 [1] (Greek) of which the transliteration is exaleipho and means (1) to anoint or wash in every part, (a) to besmear: i.e. cover with lime (to whitewash or plaster). (2) to wipe off, wipe away, (a) to obliterate, erase, wipe out, blot out.

This means that Christ not only nailed our sins to the cross as Acts 3:19 says:

"Repent therefore and be converted, that your sins may be blotted out, so that time of refreshing may come from the presence of the Lord."

It also means that our Lord also wipes away our tears because of His great victory at the Cross of Calvary and what it will mean in our redemption as Revelation 21:4 states:

"And God will wipe away every tear from their eyes; there shall be no more death, nor sorrow, nor crying. There shall be no more pain, for the former things have passed away."

Take encouragement weary traveler, the word and work of Christ is our sustainer in times of need. We may not always know what God is doing in our life, or what it is He is trying to accomplish. There may be incidences where we do not understand until many years later. We might not even find until the other side of glory because the thing God is doing might not be meant solely for us, but may be used for the next generation.

That's why He informs us that His ways and thoughts are not our ways and thoughts. We can't begin to comprehend them.

"For My thoughts are not your thoughts, nor are your ways My ways, says the LORD.

For as the heavens are higher than the earth, so are My ways higher than your ways and My thoughts than your thoughts.

For as the rain comes down, and the snow from heaven, and do not return there, but water the earth, and make it bring forth and bud, that it may give seed to the sower and bread to the eater,

So shall My word be that goes forth from My mouth; it shall not return to Me void, but it shall accomplish what I please, and it shall prosper in the thing for which I sent it." Isaiah 55:8-11

It's also why it is important when you are facing a difficulty or have a prayer project before the Lord that you ask him for a word to cling to. Then cling to it with all the tenacity that He gives you strength for. The promise is there if you do, that the word that He gives you will not come back void. It will fully succeed to that which He sent it, and it usually does so in a way that is beyond our wildest notions.

If you go back just one chapter in Isaiah to chapter 54, you will find a passage that speaks to the barrenness of life, the shame of being forsaken, grieved, and the experience of having God turn away for a moment. Isaiah is prophesying about Jerusalem's restoration, but we can certainly personalize it to be analogous to our heart wrenching situations. Read chapter 54 and walk away with the encouragement to sing in the face of adversity, knowing that God is enthroned in our praises and He can be trusted as Psalm 22:3-5 tells us:

> *"But you are holy, enthroned in the praises of Israel.*
>
> *Our fathers trusted in You; they trusted, and You delivered them.*
>
> *They cried to You, and were delivered; they trusted in You, and were not ashamed."*

Isaiah 54:4 similarly tells us not to fear for we will not be ashamed, neither disgraced, for we will not be put to shame. This verse references an even earlier verse in Isaiah 41:10 with a similar encouragement to not fear:

> *"Fear not, for I am with you; be not dismayed, for I am your God. I will strengthen you, yes, I will help you, I will uphold you with My righteous right hand."*

God is trustworthy and His word is true. When we praise Him, we invite His presence and when we trust Him, we can expect that He is going to meet our need. He may not deliver us from whatever ails us, but He promises to see us through.

Praise the God worthy of all praise in spite of the trial you may be going through right now, and know the truth of Isaiah 54:10:

> *"... His kindness shall not depart from you, nor shall His covenant of peace be removed, says the LORD, who has mercy on you."*

I encourage you to read your bible today. Take a hold of God's truth and His promises and let the Word of God accomplish His will in your life today. Your grief or sorrow may seem overwhelming at this moment, but as you begin to apply the power of Christ's finished work at the cross to your situation, healing, promise, and hope will come.

Highway of Holiness

"The truth hit me one day, ever since the accident I've walked this way."
Anonymous

The realities of life can blind side us and leave us with a stitch in our giddy up - pardon the use of an antiquated quote, but it is a fitting word picture for our journey.

Absolutely nobody foresees the hand that life deals to him or her. We don't typically start out life limping. (Those blessed with wholeness of limbs don't anyways. There are other special people that God has chosen to bear that cross, but I am speaking hypothetically). We might stub our toes a couple of times; maybe we experience a few embarrassing situations, nothing that would majorly impair our gait.

Then circumstances begin to seemingly happen to our detriment and can appear to be non-stopping.

Personally, I don't know anyone who has led a life untouched by adversity. More of what I have seen have been wounded travelers that have had children taken away from them, spouses that have left them, best friends who have betrayed them, and children who have lied to them; owners of houses that are being foreclosed, automobiles in need of repair and finances that have grown wings and taken flight.

Take heart on your journey! God has built a highway of Holiness for us. Isaiah 35:8 says:

> *"A highway shall be there, and a road, and it shall be called the Highway of Holiness. The unclean shall not pass over it, but it shall be for others. Whoever walks the road, although a fool, shall not go astray."*

The King James Version says:

> *"And an highway shall be there, and a way, and it shall be called The way of holiness; the unclean shall not pass over it, but it shall be for those the wayfaring men, though fools, shall not err therein."*

Matthew Henry beautifully elaborates on this passage of scripture in relation to Christ setting up His Kingdom in the world. He says "when our God shall come to save us he shall chalk out to us this way by his gospel, so as it had never been before described."

1. "It shall be an appointed way; not a way of sufferance, but a highway, a way into which we are directed by a divine authority and in which we are protected by a divine warrant. It is the Kings highway. The King of Kings highway, in which, though we may be waylaid, we cannot be stopped. The way of holiness is the way of God's commandments; it is (as highways usually are) the good old way, Jeremiah 6:16."

2. "It shall be an appropriated way, the way in which God will bring his own chosen to himself, but the unclean

shall not pass over it, either to defile it or to disturb those that walk in it. It is a way in itself, distinguished from the way of the world, for it is a way of separation from, and nonconformity to, this world. It shall be for those whom the Lord has set apart for himself, shall be reserved for them: The redeemed shall walk there, and the satisfaction they take in these ways of pleasantness shall be out of the reach of molestation from an evil world. The unclean shall not pass over it, for it shall be a fair way; those that walk in it are the undefiled in the way, who escape the pollution that is in the world..."

So Christ makes a way for us. He lays out a path of holiness for us to follow and then enables us to be successful in our journey. He sees everything about your life and nothing blind-sides or surprises God. He uses the good, the bad, and the ugly for His purposes.

We may walk with a bit of a limp due to life's grief, but ultimately, continuing with the thought from Matthew Henry's Commentary: "Those that keep close to this way keep out of the reach of Satan the roaring lion, that wicked one touches them not. Those that walk in the way of holiness may proceed with a holy security and serenity of mind, knowing that nothing can do them any real hurt. They shall be quiet from the fear of evil."

He that has mastery over the waves of the sea can certainly quiet the wickedness that would try to surround you. Nothing can touch the apple of His eye and if it does, it is not to our detriment, but rather for our advancement and growth in our relationship and trust of Him.

Let your way be directed today and every day with divine

authority and protected by divine warrant. Ask Christ today to let you:

> *"Stand in the ways and see, and ask for the old paths, where the good way is, and walk in it; then you will find rest for your souls..." Jeremiah 16:6*

God's Way

"What man of you, having a hundred sheep, if he loses one of them, does not leave the ninety-nine in the wilderness, and go after the one which is lost until he finds it?

And when he has found it, he lays it on his shoulders, rejoicing.

And when he comes home, he calls together his friends and neighbors, saying to them, 'Rejoice with me, for I have found my sheep which was lost!'"

Luke 15:4-6

According to the Spirit Filled Life Bible (NKJV), the author makes a note that says, "sheep that are lost lie down helplessly and refuse to budge." That makes me think that it simply does not know what to do so it lies down and waits to be found.

We have all heard the insinuations of how dumb sheep are and go figure that Christ calls us His sheep. For the most part, if we were truly honest with ourselves (and humble) we would admit this to be true.

I don't know about you, but for me one of the single most difficult things for me to do is to lie down and wait. I want to be arranging something, coordinating something, fixing something, doing something! But to just lie down and maintain trust that my Shepherd can work out my circumstances for me goes against my very nature.

Therein lays the problem. It is my nature that wars against fully trusting my person and my need to the one who has me inscribed on his hand. Isaiah 49:16:

> *"See, I have inscribed you on the palms of My hands; your walls are continually before Me."*

(I will sometimes insert the KJV translation, because as you can see from the following verse, I sometimes find the translation a bit richer in its meaning.)

> *KJV says: "Behold, I have graven thee upon the palms of my hands..."*

I went online to Webster's 1828 Dictionary [2] and looked up both words inscribed, and engraved. New versions of the dictionary will not prove to be as rewarding in meaning as when the definitions of the words were originally penned.

The definition for inscribed online said: written on; engraved; marked; addressed. This is a nice thought, kind of like going into the store in the mall called Things Remembered and picking out a trinket box for a loved one with their initials on it. Who wouldn't want to be inscribed on our Maker's hands?

But listen to the definition of engraved: Literally to scratch or scrape, hence:

1.   To cut, as metals, stones or other hard substances with

a chisel or graver; to cut figures, letters or devices, on stone or metal; to mark by incision.

Used in a sentence - Webster says: Thou shalt engrave the stones with the names of the children of Israel. Exodus 28

2. To picture or represent by incisions

3. To imprint; to impress deeply; to infix

Also an example was given in sentence: Let the laws of God and the principles of morality be engraved on the minds in early years.

(That is great advice! Not part of this story line, but heed it just the same if you have small children.)

Do you see what I mean about referring back to the King James Version? Given a choice between being inscribed into, or, graven upon my Father's hands, although each definition is wonderful, I'll take the latter. Talk about depth! You get more of a feeling of permanence, don't you?

When my son was a little guy he had a little card on his bookshelf, it had a picture of hands with a child etched on them with that scripture verse printed on the front. He loved that card and would sometimes carry it around in his bible.

Now a grown man, I came across that little card when he went off to college out of state and I sent it to him. My hope was that he would remember the rock from which he was hewn and the hands in whom he belongs and where he cannot be taken from, if he walks accordingly.

We are deeply imprinted, scarred even, into our Maker's hands.

If we follow him, lay down our agendas and do things His way, He will lead us when we need guidance, pick us up when we are lost, and shield us in the palm of His hands.

If you are lost and unsure about your way, lie down. God will pick you up, lay you on His shoulders, lead and direct your way and give you peace. He will even let you feast in the presence of your enemies when your way pleases Him.

He promises.

While We Are On
The Subject Of Sheep
(and obedience)

We had a small farm when my daughter was little. My husband brought us home a lamb our first spring there. We loved that lamb. Even though it served no purpose, since we didn't shear the wool, it was my favorite animal.

Looking back I realized that the lamb was the epitome of the symbol of trust. Will you feed me if I can't amply graze? Will you give me water? Will you keep my stall clean? Will you keep me warm and protected from the elements? Will you keep the predators away?

A lamb cannot do any of these things for itself. Especially dealing with predators. Sheep have no natural defenses.

I was able to do all for that little lamb except the last, keeping the predators away, and that was the one that proved to be fatal.

The same year that we got the lamb, after it was grown a bit, my husband decided to get another addition to our animal collection, a German Shepherd dog, Jodi. He had gotten her from strangers, advertising that she would be a good family dog, great with other animals and with children. This did not prove to be true.

While I was at work one day that dog got out, got into the lambs pen, and attacked the lamb. She died several days later due to unforeseen complications from her injuries.

Our lamb was content to be in her pen and have the family come and spend time with her. Sometimes we would let her out to stretch her legs, run around, and kick up her heels. We had bottle fed her since her birth so she was tame and we were pretty attached. Our failure was not protecting her from the wolves.

Thankfully, our God is able to do all the items on the above list that we did for the lamb AND protect us from the predators. When we trust ourselves to the one who created us and walk according to His precepts, maintaining trust that He will work out our circumstances, according to His timetable and His way, He most assuredly will come through.

I recently moved out of the comfort of familiarity, leaving my home state and family, to travel more than 1,000 miles away in the direction to which I felt the Lord leading, to bible school. At my age, leaving my hometown felt like an Abrahamic call.

Since my tendencies are to do, once I landed I fell back on my tendencies and started working on getting my resume out there, looking for a job, trying to meet people, and get established. This is not necessarily the wrong thing to do, but I knew in my heart that in my present state of affairs without any leads or connections - it had to be a God thing. God had to show me the next step.

It's in the unknown that fear tries to rear its ugly head. The enemy begins with his taunting songs. Are you currently spinning your wheels, sinking deeper in the mire with voices in every direction blaring in your head?

Let the words of one of the best-loved Psalms of all times wash over your soul.

Psalm 23

"The LORD is my shepherd; I shall not want.
He makes me to lie down in green pastures;
He leads me beside the still waters.
He restores my soul.
He leads me in the paths of righteousness for His name's sake.
Yea, though I walk through the valley of the shadow of death, I
will fear no evil;
For you are with me; Your rod and Your staff, they comfort me.
You prepare a table before me in the presence of my enemies;
You anoint my head with oil; my cup runs over.
Surely goodness and mercy shall follow me all the days of my life;
And I will dwell in the house of the LORD forever."

God will be faithful to lead and to guide you if you let Him. He does not always promise to deliver us from the hurts of life, nor from the trials. He knows how fierce they can rage against you at times. That's when He has a table prepared for you and it's filled with good things.

Daily, daily He will anoint you with the fresh oil of His spirit so that you can be renewed and refreshed to carry on. For today, make it just for today and don't let your mind travel to tomorrow, or next week, or next month.

Even though I am currently more than 1,000 miles away from where I first landed 3 months ago, I feel even as the path has been meandering, I know I am where I am supposed to be for this particular season. Psalm 107:7 says:

> *"He led them forth by the right way, that they might go to a city for a dwelling place."*

Matthew Henry says of this verse that "God always leads his people the right way; however to us it may seem circuitous; so that the furthest way about proves, if not the nearest way, yet the best way home to Canaan."

I can't tell you how confirming it was when the Lord gave me that word. We can't see the road ahead, but God can. He had to take me out of my comfort zone to an exposed place that He might try my faith. And yet, it is He that gave me the grace and strength to succeed in the trial.

> *"For it is God who works in you both to will and to do for His good pleasure." Philippians 2:13*

It is God who saves us, and it is He who continues to pour

out His spirit on us, allowing us to continue to work out our salvation and to succeed in the monotony of daily life.

What does your faith walk look like?

Do you trust the One who upholds you with His right hand and has you engraved on His hand, for the writing of your story? It is the Holy Spirit who will enable you by His great work of grace in and through you to overcome.

Voices

"That your faith should not be in the wisdom of men but in the power of God." 1 Corinthians 2:5

My dreams often have some major spiritual significance, so personal history has shown me. My problem is remembering them. The details are usually sketchy and sometimes seem to not fit together. Then I have one of those AHA moments when the Lord brings it to mind with incredible clarity and then I know what the dream represented.

This particular dream came about mid-way in my decision making process of the Abrahamic leap of faith I just mentioned. I had applied at a bible college and was having a difficult time discerning God's will as to whether or not this move was from Him.

There would be no family or friends where I was moving to, I had very little money for such a move, my car had just died an untimely death and the sea inside my head was tossing me about to and fro.

Decision-making used to be so much easier when I was younger, or so it seemed. In reality it was probably the impetuousness of youth with little regard to consequences. In a time when I should have been contemplating retirement (although I don't believe in it because I can find no biblical basis), I was contemplating uprooting my life and starting all over again.

Back to the dream...

I won't go into full detail - just the most important piece for today's message. An old friend of mine had given me a folded cellophane paper that had sewing needles in it. She also gave me a wooden configuration that looked similar to the first package. I felt impressed that the Lord said the sewing needles represented voices.

The enemy of our soul has many tricks to try and derail us. Whether those tricks come from outright curses or innocently from a friend voicing anxiety, once a seed of doubt or an anxious expression hops on board it can give license to all-out war in our minds. These are the blaring doubts, contemplative disharmony in our inner man. We can awaken one morning assured of the promise of God knowing that we are on the right track, only to be in shambles about the very decision by nightfall of the same day.

You know how it goes. Maybe you have made some bad choices in the past and family members give you that "here she goes again" look. Or you tell someone what you are planning and they ask questions like are you sure it's from God? Did He really say that?

They will tell you to look at the practical, *worldly* aspects of your decision until your mind is not where it is supposed to be (centered on God's Word) but it is trailing off down the road, 80 miles an hour on a sure crash course run.

James 1:5-8 tells us that:

> *"If any of us lack wisdom, let him ask of God, who gives*

to all liberally and without reproach, and it will be given to him.

But, (here is the great contingency) *let him ask in faith, with no doubting, for he who doubts is like a wave of the sea driven and tossed by the wind.*

For let not that man suppose that he will receive anything from the Lord; he is a double-minded man, unstable in all his ways."

After many weeks of tossing to and fro, doubting, questioning, in turmoil of mental anguish, the Lord spoke to me through this word in James and a word from Numbers 14 regarding belief. Listen to the sobering words of verse 23 in Numbers 14:

"They certainly shall not see the land of which I swore to their fathers, nor shall any of those who rejected Me see it."

In Matthew Henry's Commentary note regarding this verse it says: "Disbelief of the promise is a forfeiture of the benefit of it."

In other words, God was not only telling me be still and know that I am God, to trust and believe Him, calm the fears that were circling around in my head and not to waiver. But, He was also saying take heed, if you don't you will lose out on that which I promised you. Ouch!

That somber testimony put the fear of God in me in regards to this decision. I want to possess my inheritance through faith in the One who is faithful. I don't want to lose it due to my inherent weakness and doubts of God's ability. I believe our anxiety is really a lack of faith in God.

Here's what 1 Corinthians 2:1-5 says about where our faith should be:

> *"And I, brethren, when I came to you, did not come with excellence of speech or of wisdom declaring to you the testimony of God.*
>
> *For I determined not to know anything among you except Jesus Christ and Him crucified.*
>
> *I was with you in weakness, in fear, and in much trembling.*
>
> *And my speech and my preaching were not with persuasive words of human wisdom, but in demonstration of the Spirit and of power,*
>
> *That your faith should not be in the wisdom of men but in the power of God."*

Don't forfeit your dreams and destiny due to unbelief. Charles Spurgeon once said: "Oh brethren, be great believers! Little faith will bring your souls to heaven, but great faith will bring heaven to your souls. "

There is an excellent book written by John Piper called Faith in Future Grace. [3] He talks much about what it means to take God at His word and to look at His record in our lives of what He has done for us in the past that our faith might be empowered to know that He will continue to do for us in the future.

When making those tough decisions, or any decision for that matter, let it be the Word of God that is your decisive voice. Ask the Spirit of the Lord to lead you. Not only will He lead you, but he will also calm the stormy sea inside of your head if you let Him. Then move forward in faith.

Orchestration Of God's Plans

And the LORD went before them by day in a pillar of cloud to lead the way, and by night in a pillar of fire to give them light, so as to go by day and night. Exodus 13:21

I went off to the bible college state then unreservedly.

(Of course it wasn't as easy as I am making it sound and there's a lot more that God had to show me and do through me first, which I'll get to as the chapters progress.)

When I first told my plans of going to bible college to my best friend I told her that I might not end up there, but that in my heart I wondered if God might use it as a spring board to get me to a difference place, a place of promise to show me His glory. Hopefully through the experience I would be able, by His grace of course, to show His glory through me.

Your perspective changes when you remain in the place of trust and faith with God. You move knowing that God is totally in control, not so much as a determined place of - I just made the decision, but a place where events just seem to flow together in perfect harmony with ease. Let me give you a personal illustration.

Hannah Rose

The Carolinas eastern seacoast is perhaps my favorite place on earth thus far. I would often take my children camping there during our summer time together.

All three of us loved the water and the sand. Our trips to the coast were typically filled with my children begging me to look harder up and down the beaches for the perfect spot. One that had a wall of rocks where they could don snorkels and dive underwater near the rocks looking for wonders to behold.

During one of our trips my children and I were engaged in one of our favorite activities of beach combing when the clouds began to darken ever so slightly. If any of you are familiar with a storm coming up from the sea, it can happen quickly and sometimes with little warning.

The three of us were looking for treasures, each of us a bit of a distance away from the next, but still within line of sight. It began to rain very lightly and slowly. You would feel a drop here, then another one there, but nothing in steady succession. After feeling the first few drops each one of us turned back toward the direction of where we had left our stuff. Our heads still pointed down, eyes intently studying the sand, not willing to forfeit any potential treasure find.

As the rain began to sprinkle a bit more slowly but steadily, my children moved closer toward me and all three of us just naturally fell in line to gather our gear and head toward the car. None of us said a word, we just all acted in unison and by the time we were in the safety of the car, the storm hit full force.

If any of you have experienced the severity of a Carolina rainstorm, you know what I am talking about. Even windshield wipers at full force can't contend with the velocity of the drops.

Our walking in one accord as a family is how I view walking in faith. One of our pastors of the church we belonged to at that time told me that he saw my two children and I as a symphony. I thought that was a beautiful compliment. Sometimes as a single mom some of your days might feel a little less than harmonic.

Our beach experience was an expression of how we moved together back then. It's a great example of how to move with God, to trust Him to maintain your path, knowing full well He is able to keep you and when you need to go in a different direction or make a decision, you are going to do it with an inner peace that passes all understanding and one that doesn't necessarily require a lot of discourse. You'll just know that you know.

There are many days that I would love a visible cloud or pillar of fire to show me the way. How fun would that be to show up at your work place with? It would turn a few heads, wouldn't it? We have something even better if we have the Spirit of God residing in us!

My prayer for you today reader, is that as you ask God for wisdom in your decision making, your answer would be as clear as the clouds in the sky, or as visible as a pillar of fire in your darkness. And, that in your inner being you would just know that you know.

Vessels of Honor In The Making

The word which came to Jeremiah from the LORD, saying:

> *"Arise and go down to the potter's house, and there I will cause you to hear My words."*

> *Then I went down to the potter's house, and there he was, making something at the wheel.*

> *And the vessel that he made of clay was marred in the hand of the potter; so he made it again into another vessel, as it seemed good to the potter to make.*

Then the word of the LORD came to me, saying:

> *"O house of Israel, can I not do with you as this potter?" says the LORD. "Look, as the clay is in the potter's hand, so are you in My hand, O house of Israel!"*

> *Jeremiah 18:1-6*

This word out of Jeremiah witnessed to my heart and the Lord used to further my understanding of the implicitness of His ways.

I had been thinking often of what I thought was the original purpose of this book, to unfold a faith journey that began in the depth of indecisive despair and resulted in obtaining a Father's promise.

My original goal to attend bible school ended in a move to Memphis, TN, and having thus landed a new objective, I felt a bit silly continuing because the story line had changed. Thing is, the only story line that changed was mine, not God's.

I read in the Westminster Confession of Faith [4] regarding God's eternal decree, and things that happen a particular way because God ordains them so. It had been so difficult for me to wrap my mind around this because somewhere along the line prior teachings had me to believe that God ordains a particular thing, but due to man's free will we can mess it up, slow it down, or miss, God's perfect design.

This is contrary to what the Confession of Faith teaches:

> *"God from all eternity did, by the most holy and wise counsel of his own will, freely and unchangeably ordain whatsoever comes to pass. God foresees with certainty only because he guarantees the certainty."*

> God's word tells us in *Ephesians 1:11: "In Him also we have obtained an inheritance being predestined according to the purpose of Him who works all things according to the counsel of His will."*

Read that whole first chapter of Ephesians if you need to get some clarity of God's sovereignty.

Sure our ideas or understanding of God's plans might change, because we are finite and don't operate with God's wisdom. But His ordinations stand.

My plan hadn't changed that dramatically, because ultimately in my heart I knew that my trip to Florida might be a springboard idea for God to get me where He wanted me. At the same time making the changes He saw fit (and continues to see fit) to make in me. In Christ we are continually being changed from glory to glory.

Out of my love for Christ and my desire to learn all that I can about Him, study to show myself approved, and have answers to defend my faith, in my logic, bible school was the answer. Use the vessel I am and fill it. This made sense to me, but apparently God had different plans of molding me this season.

The Lord tells Jeremiah in verse 2 to

> *"Arise and go down to the potter's house, and there I will cause thee to hear my words."*

I just want to pause there for a moment.

The Lord was already speaking and Jeremiah was already listening when the Lord told him to go to the potter's house. When I was in New York, the Lord was already speaking to me, I heard him. I wanted to be obedient, as absolutely horrifying as it seemed to me at the time. I don't want to miss a blessing, so I go where I feel God is leading, and I hear Him.

But then I hear God in a new way. More importantly I experienced Him in a new way. He taught me to whole-heartedly trust that in the darkest times and bleakest places. He promised to be my shield, capable of covering my entire body, my exceedingly great reward! The Lord took me from a very depressed and oppressive place, out into the open with no cover and no one to lean on except Him, and He proved himself to me in such a way that removed all fear and anxiety.

Returning to the Jeremiah story, in verse 3 (KJV)

> *"Then I went down to the potter's house, and, behold, he wrought a work on the wheels. And the vessel that he made of clay was marred in the hand of the potter; so he made it again another vessel, as seemed good to the potter to make it.* Then in verse 6 the Lord says to Jeremiah: *"O house of Israel, cannot I do with you as this potter? saith the LORD. Behold, as the clay is in the potter's hand, so are ye in mine hand, O house of Israel."*

The scriptural reference to "cannot I do with you" is Isaiah 45:9, was the very section of scripture that at the time I had been studying at the time:

> *"Woe to him who strives with his Maker! Let the potsherd strive with the potsherds of the earth! Shall the clay say to him who forms it, 'What are you making?' Or shall your handiwork say, "He has no hands""?*

Yes, God could have given Jeremiah the message in words without showing him the vessel in the making. Just as He could have spoken to me in New York to go to Tennessee, bypassing the Florida jaunt. But I would have missed what God needed me to experience as He continues to mold the vessel that He is creating of me. He's God. He can do whatever He pleases. And He loves us enough to know and give us exactly what He knows that we need to grow and mature in Him.

In your daily walk today with your Maker, reflect His love for you in your heart in all you do. Rest assured in your surrender to Christ.

He is making a beautiful thing in you.

Excuses, Stutters, Procrastinations, And Thorns

It had been a while since my last writing entry when God brought to the forefront of my mind a couple of issues that he wanted to free me of, directly relating to having put my pen down.

I had started writing this piece of literature with all the tenacity and force that I could muster. Initially excited at the prospect of speaking God's message and healing word to weary sojourners, but then I stopped.

Granted I moved and took on a full time job. I came to settle in with my daughter who I had not seen in a very long time, and who had been newly married to man that I didn't know. So spending time with my daughter and getting to know my son-in-law took first place on the priority list.

When I had started this project I had nothing else going on. No job to attend to, and I had lots of time on my hands. I wondered if somehow God would use this for provision in my life. Then, with moving out of state and getting a new job, the project seemed less important. Unconsciously, two other things were also happening.

God took me back to a point of impact in my childhood that had affected me profoundly and was having an effect on what little progress I was making now.

We had grown up with very little and consequently I was not well read but I enjoyed the few books that I had. The church that I grew up in used to have a rack in back of it with bible stories. Every now and then my mom would get me one and I would read those books over and over.

You know when you are a little kid and people ask what you want to be when you grow up? Well my very first desire was to be an author. I'm not quite sure why, perhaps I thought it might be a good way to get more books.

Anyway, I was very young and extremely shy. Back in the day of my youth, growing up in the city meant that everyone knew everyone else on the block and all the kids played together, cutting through hedge row and creeping under fences to get to each other's yards. One day, a mother of one of the kids that I was playing with asked me what I wanted to be when I grew up. The child I was playing with, although they lived in back of us, was more of an acquaintance than a good friend, so I barely knew the mom.

By the way, speaking from experience, if a shy child is asked a question from a person they barely know, it is a social nightmare. What goes through your mind is just about everything else except the answer. If you do manage to spit it out it takes all that you can give to be able to respond.

Reservedly I answer her that I want to write books. I'm sure her follow up question was an honest one. Keeping in line with making conversation she asks if I was good at grammar or favored English, or something of consequence if you are going to write books for a living. However, I had no idea what she was asking me, got embarrassed, and told her I didn't know what she meant. Her response, obviously thinking I was dim-witted was that maybe I wanted to get a handle on language arts before I banked on a career that depended upon it.

It doesn't take an extroverted, socially well - adjusted child to know when someone is poking fun at them, but my feelings weren't really hurt until I found out what she meant. At that point I don't think I ever, ever gave a thought to writing books again until this endeavor.

Additionally another deterrent occurred when I was in a Florida bookstore shortly after beginning this book. I was looking at the aisles of devotionals. (Note: Don't ever do that if you are attempting to write something similar. There are so many out there you are sure that yours will be trunk fodder for your automobile.)

(Ha, jokes on whomever, I don't currently own a car!)

Seriously though, a woman in the next aisle over was talking on the phone said loudly, "yes! They have an excellent selection of devotionals. It's overwhelming; there are over 3 aisles!!! " I don't think, I know I took that as a negative statement to my heart and subconsciously figured just that, who in their right mind would consider writing one more!

As the Lord began to blow the dust off of my previously written pages He gave me a word out of Deuteronomy 8:18:

> *"And you shall remember the LORD your God, for it is He who gives you power to get wealth, that He may establish His covenant which He swore to your fathers, as it is this day."*

The study bible that I have previously mentioned and was using at the time has a tool called word wealth and gave the meaning of the word "power: Koach (Ko-akh) means vigor, strength, force, capacity or ability, whether physical, mental or spiritual. Here Moses informs Israel that it is God who gives them the ability, (power, means, endurance, capacity) to obtain wealth, for material blessings are included in the promises to the patriarchs and their descendants.

Moses strictly warns Israel in verse 17 not to falsely conclude that this capacity for success is an innate talent, but to humbly acknowledge that it is a God-given ability."

I'm all about my children's and my purpose and destinies being fulfilled.

And it's all God.

I believe that God was initiating with this writing a beautiful message for whatever He uses it for, personally spiritual or physcial; provision, fire kindling, a paperweight, or for my own personal look back. I hope it's more than that. I hope that this book inspires others to know that:

> *"It is God who works in you both to will and to do for His good pleasure." Philippians 2:13*

I was allowing weeds to get in and choke God's work. Enemy voices of discouragement and pride were rearing their ugly heads saying I'm too busy - put that idea back on the shelf. I even reminded the Lord that I didn't have the proper tools. My study bible, commentary, and dictionaries were in my hometown packed in storage. I had no computer; and I had no transportation to get to the public library for research and computer use.

But a transforming thing happened when I finally borrowed my daughter's car to go the library to see what kind of reference materials and/or books of interest they had that I could use. I'm going to digress momentarily, but I will bring it all back around. I promise.

Part of my coming to Tennessee was my daughter had a job waiting for me. I had spent the better part of two years unemployed and desperately seeking God about employment. The good thing about the job in Tennessee is that it is cleaning and working in an office part time. I love doing both. The bad thing is that I turned 50 this year and so the initial month of 30 hours or more per week of cleaning seemed to be taking their toll. I was slightly surprised because I am in decent shape, but my back was killing me and that was new. After I broke every curse known to man, I sought the Lord regarding and He reminded me that sometimes He gives a thorn in the side (2 Corinthians 12:7-10) (and back and knees)as a reminder to press into and lean only upon Him.

I had shared with my daughter that I was always afraid if I had money I would forget to rely totally upon my Lord and Maker. Seeing as how as of the writing of this page, after just having written the rent check, my checking account is overdrawn by almost two hundred dollars, it doesn't look like surplus money is going to be an issue.

But obedience was.

As I began writing again, I could feel a dramatic reduction in pain. I immediately knew that the LORD was healing me. Anybody who has ever suffered from a raw sciatic nerve or twisted/swollen nerve pain knows that it does not suddenly withdraw itself unless God is at work. The next morning as I went to get off my roll on the floor I was about 75% better. At work that day I would say that I was stiff, but not in pain.

The only tools that I truly need are a pen and paper and God's word. He was looking to me to fully rely on Him for this endeavor and I put it on a shelf.

How irreverent of me.

The Lord has promised good to me. He gave me a thorn so that I would seek Him as to the source so that ultimately I would come to Him in my time of need and receive His grace to bear up and find mercy in His healing. He reminds me that He will fulfill His purpose and destiny for me if I will follow.

The Lord had to get me past the entire world's no's to His yes. To submit to the purpose that He has for me instead of what my idea was.

Have you asked the Lord what your purpose or destiny is? Would you like to know how He could use you? God would like to help you develop the gifts and talents that He has given you to bring Him glory.

If you never have I encourage you to spend some time and ask the Holy Spirit to help you discern your gifts and how you can use the for the furtherance of Christ's Kingdom. If you haven't been on top of your game, or you have let the cob webs settle in your life, dust them off and let God revitalize your work for Him.

Psalm 28 is a fitting Psalm to insert here. It speaks of regarding God's work and having reverence for Him. And of having a posture of praise.

"To You I will cry, O LORD my Rock; do not be silent to me, lest, if You are silent to me, I become like those who go down to the pit.

Hear the voice of my supplications when I cry to You, when I life up my hands toward Your holy sanctuary.

Do not take me away with the wicked and with the workers of iniquity, who speak peace to their neighbors, but evil is in their hearts.

Give them according to their deeds, and according to the wickedness of their endeavors; give them according to the work of their hands; render to them what they deserve.

Because they do not regard the works of the LORD, nor the operation of His hands, He shall destroy them and not build them up.

Blessed be the LORD, because He has heard the voice of my supplications!

The LORD is my strength and my shield; my heart trusted in Him, and I am helped; therefore my heart greatly rejoices, and with my song I will praise Him.

The LORD is their strength and He is the saving refuge of His anointed.

Save Your people, and bless Your inheritance; shepherd them also, and bear them up forever."

Foundation And Roots

Once the idea of authorship was dead for me at the age of 5, all that I wanted most from then on was to be married and have children. I would imagine a man who loved and was devoted to me, whom I loved in the same manner living in a big house full of children.

There was a time in my life that I would say life cheated me, but I now see that through a series of wrong choices, not having a relationship with Christ in my earlier years, and living in a fallen world, the only thing that got the short end of the stick was living my life for Christ early on. In His faithfulness God has used and continues to use my experiences and my former pain as an instrument of refining.

Prior to giving birth to my daughter I had absolutely no idea that you could possibly love anybody as much as I loved her. She was at death's door at the time of her birth and we almost lost her. I begged God not to take her from me and made a bargain with Him that if He were going to take her, could He please at least give me five years with her?

A ridiculous bargain and plea, I know. But at the time I knew only there was a God; I didn't understand the concept of trusting Him with my life, much less my child's life.

It was a tough go those early years, although she was completely whole, healthy, and developmentally fine, she was colicky and only weighing 4 pounds at birth, she needed to nurse constantly and be reassured of my presence continually as she grew.

Thankfully the good Lord did not take her from when she was five. He has great plans yet unfolded for her. When she was 4 1/2 years old, God blessed me with a son. During my pregnancy I was fearful that I would not have any love left over for him. Of course when he was born, naturally I did. Through the years I have realized the capacity God gives us for unconditional love of our children in huge magnitude.

I was a wife and I was a mom. My children were the apple of my eye. I rearranged my life, seeking a career to work around my children. They were the center of my life.

Through a series of misfortunate events and what I consider to be an unjust legal system, I lost custody of my children. The most significant piece of me was taken. I came undone and it nearly sent me to the brink of suicide.

Thankfully I had met the Lord prior to the outcome of divorce proceedings, because if I had not had a relationship with Jesus I would most certainly have been hopeless and not have wanted to, nor have seen the sense of continuing life.

The roots that we had put down as a husband and wife with our children were completely destroyed. Life was not, and never has been the same.

Many times over the years I have felt the Lord tell me He is re-establishing my root system. And with each move to a new residence or area that I make I've thought, well that's not the place where the Lord wanted to plant me, to let my roots sink deep in the soil and take place. And I've been right. These aren't the places because that wasn't my message. I've realized with the trials of life that I have learned to trust Jesus unconditionally. I have learned about God's power. How as in *Deuteronomy 33:26:*

> *"There is no God like the God of Jeshuran, who rides the heavens to help you, and in His excellency on the clouds.*
>
> *The eternal God is your refuge, and underneath are the everlasting arms; He will thrust out the enemy from before you, and will say, Destroy!"*

My roots weren't to reach anywhere but to the depth of Christ's fertile soil and His loving care.

In God's Word, Isaiah 6 tells of that terrifying and awe inspiring commissioning of Isaiah and ends the chapter with God prophesying a time of desolation in the land. But, in verse 13, He encourages the prophet:

> *"But yet in it shall be a tenth, and it shall return, and shall be eaten as a teil tree, and as an oak, whose substance is in the, when they cast their leaves so the holy seed shall be the substance thereof." (KJV)*

The scripture reference for Isaiah 6:13 is Job 14:7 which reads:

> *"For there is hope of a tree, if it be cut down, that it will sprout again, and that the tender branch thereof will not cease." (KJV)*

Matthew Henry's Commentary regarding this verse states "that the holy seed in the soul is the substance of man: a principle of grace reigning in the heart will keep life there; he that is born of God has his seed remaining in him."

The Lord has pruned me back to a stump these past 20 years or so, to show me that life, His life, grows out of devastation and pain and flourishes, abounding with grace.

The place of my physical existence doesn't matter, except being where God wants me to be so that His purposes can unfold. We weren't meant to root into the soil of this world, but rather the importance is our spiritual soil and root system and cultivating a godly life on His vine.

Have you felt out of place in this life and in your circumstances? This can happen even with our friends and family members. I believe it's God's way of reminding us that our worth comes from Him and our dependence should be upon Him for the most essential of our needs. Also, that this world is not our home.

Don't get caught up in the trappings of this life, but remember the analogy of a plant and let your root system grow upward to your relationship with Christ, and not downward into a life that ultimately cannot satisfy.

Giving It All Up For The Cause Of Christ?

"Do not lay up for yourselves treasures on earth, where moth and rust destroy and where thieves break in and steal;

But lay up for yourselves treasures in heaven where neither moth nor rust destroys and where thieves do not break in and steal.

For where your treasure is, there your heart will be also."
Matthew 6:19-21

"Labour not to be rich, cease from thine own wisdom."
Proverbs 23:4 (KJV)

"Do not overwork to be rich; because of your own understanding, cease!" Proverbs 23:4 (NKJV)

"Charge them that are rich in this world, that they not be high minded, nor trust in uncertain riches, but in the living God, who giveth us richly all things to enjoy." 1 Timothy 6:17

Matthew Henry says of the Matthew 6 reference: "Worldly-mindedness is as common and as fatal a symptom of hypocrisy as any other, for by no sin can Satan have a surer and faster hold of the soul, under the cloak of a visible and passable profession of religion than by this; and therefore Christ having warned us against coveting the praise of men, proceeds next to warn us against coveting the wealth of the world..."

When I was first married and pregnant for my daughter, my age of 25 was not indication of maturity, nor of self-assurance. I was personally insecure and so afraid of what others thought of me. My need for acceptance was deeper than a well.

My husband had successfully finished school and was grounded in a career. His many like-minded friends were in the same status. When asked what school I graduated from or what I did for a living, I was always tremendously embarrassed that I had not graduated from college. I would justify, or try to, with reasons why I had dropped out and changed majors only to drop out again. Usually the excuses would be followed up with grandiose ideas of what I intended to do.

That is, if ever those full sentences came out of my mouth. My timidity kept me away from most social situations and so those conversations were few and far between. However, the stigma and self-imposed judgment and sting of insecurity of what others thought of me, remained in the forefront of my mind.

Eventually, after my divorce I did have a successful administrative career, orchestrated by a loving God. I also went on to complete my degrees both in undergraduate and graduate school.

At one point I was on top of the world. This temporal, ever changing, unfriendly to Christ's-own, world that is. I had an excellent career, new car, and a beautiful home (by my standards). My house was tastefully decorated with my treasures and furniture of my choosing. I was attending school for my master's degree. I communicated daily with my daughter, who was out of state attending music school, and saw my son regularly, who lived nearby.

I was semi-content. Sure there were student loans, credit card statements, mortgage payments, a car loan and house hold expenditures to worry about daily. But I was careful so that my house of cards did not topple down. Until it did. And it did in a bad way.

At this point in my young life I was in my mid-forties and both my parents were deceased. There is a great void in your life at any age when you don't have your parents to lean on, even if just for a bit of emotional support. I was pretty much the center of my own world even though I thought at the time that God was.

As I hand-pen this on a notebook purchased at a local department store, I sit on a memory foam roll on the floor that serves as my bed. I do not own a bed and even the linens on the roll are not mine. However, I am surround by God's word (2 bibles), an online reference commentary (even though I'm reading it on the tiny screen of my cell phone which keeps cutting out), and my hand written index cards with scripture verses that I can pull out at any time of the day and help me remember all that Christ is for me and has done for me. Most importantly I am surrounded by God's Spirit in this dark world. And I am content. In fact, I am more content and at peace that at any other time of my life.

Why? Because I have nothing else in this world except Christ, but Christ is all we need.

Did I willingly give up all for the cause of Christ? How saintly that would have been if I had. The answer is of course no. Christ in His manifold wisdom, by and with great measures of His grace, enabled me to be extricated from the trappings of lies of this life. I know it is not wrong to desire a husband and children, or a nice home and stability. But that is not the end all. Many people have exactly what they sought after in this life and are unfulfilled to the very core of their being.

One by one and over time, I lost just about everything I took personal pride in or received accolades from. Christ allowed them to be taken. He is not a vindictive God who takes pleasure in our loss and pain. He is a holy God who loves me enough to know what I need and He has literally gone to great pains to insure my eternal salvation and that my eyes stay focused on what's important, Him.

What is at the center of your heart? Do you have the courage to ask God to give you eyes to see what's important to Him, instead of to you? Are you willing to be honest with yourself, right now to ask the Lord to remove from you anything that exalts itself in your heart over Him?

If you do, I can almost guarantee that you will be surprised at what He shows you, and it might be more difficult to let go of than you thought.

Go ahead and do it though, it's better than the benefits of carrots for your eyesight, and the release your soul will experience when you do lay down any idols will be invaluable.

Trappings Of This Life

A problem remains in me then that these trappings could snare me again. Not that I haven't learned my lesson or that I love God any less, but because I'm fallible and human, living in a fallen world.

That is why Christ encourages to guard our heart with all diligence because out of it springs the issues of life. Also because I am a work in progress, and will be until the day that I die.

And providence is a continued creation. (That's a Matthew Henry thought.)

As I was writing this I looked over at my bedside table. I have sitting next to my lamp a quote that reads, "Mercy first and last shall brightest shine." I can't remember where I read that, but the biblical text that I have referenced underneath it is Hosea 14:1-9. It is an excellent synopsis of what I feel the Lord is leading me to say. For this reference I am using the NIV translation [5]

"Return, O Israel, to the LORD your God. Your sins have been your downfall!

Take words with you and return to the LORD. Say to him "Forgive all our sins and receive us graciously, that we may offer the fruit of our lips.

Assyria cannot save us; we will not mount war-horses. We will never again say 'Our gods' to what our own hands have made, for in you the fatherless find compassion.

I will heal their waywardness and love them freely, for my anger has turned away from them.

I will be like the dew to Israel; he will blossom like a lily. Like a cedar of Lebanon he will send down his roots;

His young shoots will grow. His splendor will be like an olive tree, his fragrance like a cedar of Lebanon.

Men will dwell again in his shade. He will blossom like a vine and his fame will be like the wine from Lebanon.

(*The NKJV translates verse 7 as this: "Those who dwell under his shadow shall return; they shall be revived like grain, and grow like a vine. Their scent shall be like the wine of Lebanon.")*

O Ephraim, what more have I to do with idols? I will answer him and care for him. I am like a green pine tree; your fruitfulness comes from me."

Who is wise? He will realize these things. Who is discerning? He will understand them. The ways of the LORD are right; the righteous walk in them, but the rebellious stumble in them."

Therein lies the answer to my concern of the trappings of this world getting a hold on my soul again. God shows us in the passage of Hosea that when we repent of our sin He will restore us and uses rich symbolism out of his provision in nature to make His point. That he will be like the dew to us, we will be beautiful like the lily to Him. He alone will give us stability as we take root and we will bear fruit, enabling us to be a sweet fragrance to Him, as He provides us with shade.

What rich language. May our souls drink in His promises!

My earlier reference of not having parents is also addressed here. In the KJ version of this passage there is a reference in verse 3 to Psalm 10:14:

> *"But You have seen, for You observe trouble and grief, to repay it by Your hand. The helpless commits himself to You; You are the helper of the fatherless."*

God loves us to be surrounded by loving relationships, but when we lack to necessary support, He provides.

Listen to similar words in Psalm 68:5&6:

> *"A father of the fatherless, a defender of widows, is God in His holy habitation.*
>
> *God sets the solitary in families; he brings out those who are bound into prosperity; but the rebellious dwell in a dry land."*

The last sentence is sobering and quite the opposite of the beautiful language we heard in Hosea promises of blessing for those who repent.

I'm thankful that when I am weak, God is strong. He promises me that when I come to Him with questions of how to maneuver the paths in this life, He is quick to answer and assure me that if I fall, He will pick me up. But not only will He pick me up, He will bless me beyond belief and send me the support that I need,

Hannah Rose

just when I need it. I take comfort that I don't need to look to anything or anyone else to fulfill my longings. He does it all.

I encourage you to lay down the work of your hands and let the Father of the fatherless show you His compassion in a tangible way.

Seasons

It is such an incredible blessing to be with my daughter and son-in-law and to finally be employed.

I am the self appointed dog walker to their two amazing dogs, and I also pitch in helping to clean up around the house. We are now into the Christmas season and although I don't buy into the materialism of the season, I do purchase some gifts. Strategically planning to shop and the holiday planning now take up additional time. Then there will be shipping of the gifts and holiday baking to be done.

These are all objects of desire that tug at the strings of my heart, vying for my time and attention. This is time and attention that deserve to be spent with my King and which during my seasons of unemployment were.

Seasons are what the Lord just reminded me of. Seasons and the moments contained within them will wax and wane and although I am always in Christ and He is always near me, sometimes my attention is diverted elsewhere.

I had been busy this past week, working on a homemade Christmas gift for my sister that requires a lot of my time. The busyness of life had begun to crowd on the time that I typically would spend in devotions, reading my bible, studying, memorizing (or trying to), worshiping and listening for God's still small voice.

I sat in my room thinking that when my back had been bothering me. During that painful time I was medicating daily with Tylenol, stretching, and using the exercise ball for sit-ups, just to make it through the day for work.

God spoke to me about the trials that He allows me to go through and how He uses them to draw me closer to Him. He gave me a great analogy using the example of what I was physically doing for my body to encourage me to do it for my spirit. He showed me that the times of trials are used to draw me closer to Him. It is during the time of pain and adversity when I am most prone to spend time in His presence. Pressing into Him; seeking, searching, and medicating my soul; exercising my spirit; stretching my inner being - straining to hear; running my race like an athlete.

It's not that I love God any less during the busy seasons, He knows. But He also is jealous for my time and attention. I think He wants me to reflect on the goodness and the blessings that come out of the trying times so that when I press in, He gives me treasures of darkness and hidden riches of secret places. So that I will know that He, the Lord, who calls me by my name, is the God of Israel.

When Paul experienced his thorn in the flesh in 2 Corinthians 12:7-10, the Lord's answer to him after he asked Him to remove it was:

> *"My grace is sufficient for you, for My strength is made perfect in weakness."*

God gives us opportunities in this life to meet a new characteristic of Himself that we had not met before. If we can enter into our different seasons with this perspective it makes the journey a lot more enjoyable.

Have there been seasons of darkness in your life where you just couldn't see the road ahead? Maybe the trial didn't make sense or the pain seemed too intense for you. Perhaps you are in that season right now. Do not be discouraged but rather be encouraged by God's word and the nearness of our Father. He never moves away, but we do.

Press into His presence through His Word and prayer because it is there that He will uncover those treasure troves that had before been hidden from you. This may be the time that you will be able to access them. When you begin to find them, when you begin to say Lord God your presence is more important to me than all else, everything else will eventually be righted.

Don't lie down! Lace us those running shoes of the spirit and run the race set before you!

In Luke chapter 13:22 Jesus was going *"through the cities and villages, teaching and journeying toward Jerusalem.*

> *Then one said to Him, "Lord, are there few who are saved?" And He said to them,*

> *"Strive to enter through the narrow gate, for many, I say to you, will seek to enter and will not be able."*

John Piper in his book *Future Grace* references this passage and defines the word strive as agonizomai. It means struggle or contend for victory like an athlete.

Matthew Henry speaks of the difficulty of entering heaven as "a point that will not be gained without a great deal of care and pains, of difficulty and diligence. We must strive with God in prayer, wrestle as Jacob, strive against sin and Satan."

"We must strive in every duty of religion; strive with our own hearts, agonizethe - be in agony: strive as those that run for a prize, excite and exert ourselves to the utmost."

There is nothing lax about how we are supposed to approach our Christian walk. I think the mistake that far too many Christians make is taking God's grace for granted and thinking, because He is such a loving Father, that He will understand all the don'ts of our life. If we don't press in, in prayer; if we don't read His word daily; if we don't discipline our bodies and bring the flesh under control of the Spirit; if we don't seek Him for sanctification.

Yes, He is a loving Father. Yes, He understands our weaknesses. However, remember first and foremost my brother or sister in Christ, He is Holy and we, representing Him also need to be a holy, separate only unto Him, His sanctified people.

Make it your motto today to Strive For The Prize!!

Not By Might

This past week the Lord has been speaking to me about His power in the Spirit. He brought to mind a number of verses, one of them a favorite of mine in Zechariah 4:6&7

> *"So he answered and said to me: "This is the word of the LORD to Zerubbabel: 'Not by might nor by power, but by My Spirit', says the LORD of hosts.*
>
> *'Who are you, O great mountain? Before Zerubbabel you shall become a plain! and he shall bring forth the capstone with shouts of "Grace, grace to it!""""*

The note in my study bible says: "When the temple is completed, all will acknowledge its beauty and realize it is not the result of human achievements, but rather of God's grace and more grace. O great mountain could be the opposition of adversaries of the temple project, the discouraged group of builders, or some type of turmoil among the people. At any rate, God shall see to it that it shall become a plain. The New Testament (NT) use of "mountain" and Zechariah's obvious allusion to Isaiah 40:4 (which says:

> *"Every valley shall be exalted and every mountain and hill brought low; the crooked places shall be made straight and the rough places smooth;),* make this a future promise

as well. The Messiah's future NT reign will see the removal of many "mountains" by God's grace."

After years of discouragement, Zerubbabel is assured that He will see the fulfillment of God's purpose for him. Verse 9 goes on to say:

"The hands of Zerubbabel have laid the foundation of the temple; his hands shall also finish it, then you will know that the LORD of hosts has sent Me to you."

The author of *How The Gospel Brings Us All The Way Home*, Derek W. H. Thomas [6] writes: "Every believer lives in a tension between what he is and what he will be, between the now and not yet and God the Holy spirit is intimately involved at each stage.

Now - the Holy Spirit dwells in the body, giving life (Romans 8:10).

Not yet - the Holy Spirit will raise the body to (resurrection) life (Romans 8:11).

The presence of the Holy Spirit in us now is the "guarantee of our inheritance until we acquire possession of it" (Ephesians 1:14).

This speaks to me on two fronts, the earthly and the eternal. To some degree the tension that I experience in my mind is completely normal. This life, because it is the here and now, the physical, occupies my mind (or tries to) and I try to bring it back to concentrate on Christ (unseen, infinite, spiritual matters). It is also an expected event because I am human. But we were made in Christ's image as spiritual beings first and as such have a mandate to follow after the things of the Spirit.

Part of this also speaks about my inheritance, which I have been looking at from a temporal, physical perspective. My inheritance is in Christ, life in the Spirit and eternity. That's where I need to dwell. Period. What am I doing today that will reverberate forever?

I have suffered profound losses in my life and have looked to God for what I believe have been promises of restoration. My desire for these promises is not sinful or ungodly. I've already mentioned that. I believe God has put those desires in my heart so that He will get the glory when they are fulfilled.

But God has spoken to me about the fact that I can have something and not possess it - that is the Spirit within me - He is my guarantee of my inheritance in the resurrected life. God brought me to a place to trust solely in Him purposefully and in the power of His Spirit of grace. That is the mindset that we are to have.

I have questioned that maybe the story of Job is also a shadow and type. In other words, maybe God wants to use the story of Job's restoration symbolically as a picture of the afterlife and His blessing in the latter part of Job's life was supposed to represent the blessing of his life in eternity. But even as I write this I realize this is not entirely so. That God does in fact have good things for us now, not just in eternity. We just can't let them rule us.

The Psalmist said in Psalm 80:7:

> *"Restore us, O God of hosts; cause Your face to shine, and we shall be saved!"*

Is there a piece of your life, a part of your story that you have asked the LORD to restore or believe that He has spoken to you about? If there is, believe, and then trust in the God that can level mountains. He will do what He has told you He will do, and that which He is more than capable of doing.

Your part is to speak to your mountain. Is your mountain debt? Is it a loved one? Personal persecution? Failed relationships? Speak grace in faith to those mountains and remember, that it is not by might, nor by power, but by the Spirit of the Lord.

Then watch those mountains fall.

Possess AND Own

"...For this purpose the Son of God was manifested, that He might destroy the works of the devil." 1 John 3:8

I recently revisited a book that I read many years ago. The particular chapter that I was reading was about the Holy Spirit. Ever notice that when God wants your attention on a particular matter He will deliver the message to you in various, multiple ways in a very fulfilling, life breathing manner?

God was continuing to teach me that my ineffectiveness and weakness was from walking in my own strength and not trusting His Spirit in and for all things. After reading the aforementioned chapter, I confessed to the Lord that I am so weak and seemingly ineffectual. I long for my Father's voice and presence, dreams and visions. Almost immediately I felt impressed to memorize Psalm 3:

> *"LORD, how they have increased who trouble me! Many are they who rise up against me.*
>
> *Many are they who say of me, "There is no help for him in God." Selah*
>
> *But You, O LORD, are a shield for me, my glory and the One who lifts up my head.*

> *I cried to the LORD with my voice, and He heard me from His holy hill. Selah*
>
> *I lay down and slept; I awoke, for the LORD sustained me.*
>
> *I will not be afraid of ten thousands of people who have set themselves against me all around.*
>
> *Arise, O LORD; save me, O my God! For You have struck all my enemies on the cheekbone; You have broken the teeth of the ungodly.*
>
> *Salvation belongs to the LORD. Your blessing is upon Your people. Selah"*

As I memorized this Psalm, I was taken with the fact that He's not saying that He will strike all my enemies on the cheekbone - He already has. And it doesn't say He is going to break the teeth of the ungodly, it says He's already done it. To break the teeth means to render powerless. God is not just thinking about doing this, pouring forth His power to deal with our enemies or pouring forth His grace to us so that we can defeat them if the enemies happen to be internal - He's already done it.

In the book *Intercessory Prayer* [7] Dutch Sheets says:

"We don't deliver anyone, we don't reconcile anyone to God, and we don't defeat the enemy. The work is already done. Reconciliation is complete. Deliverance and victory are complete. Salvation is complete. Intercession is complete! Finished! Done!"

The enemies we fight with, both internal such as addictions, doubt, worry, fear...as well as external: rejection, prejudices, injustices, etc...are already defeated. Christ's sacrifice on the cross, obtained our victory over death, disease, and sin.

God was expounding one of His former lessons to me regarding the possibility of owning something and not possessing it. In his book, Dutch relates a story about a girl in a village chained to a tree. God told Dutch to pray for her - to represent Him and break the powers of darkness so that the villagers would know Dutch was preaching the truth to them. He reminds us that the emphasis is always on the One who sends us, that God has chosen to work through His people, and that God assigned responsibility - We are His spokesmen.

"Jesus is the victor - we are the enforcers.

Jesus is the redeemer - we are the releasers.

Jesus is the head - we are the body."

(Intercessory Prayer)

Our prayers of intercession release Christ's finished work of intercession. We possess through God's Spirit, all the power to intercede for others to see Christ's work in their lives. We have that power within us if we have accepted Jesus as our Lord and Savior. The very power that healed the sick and brought the dead back to life resides within us. 1 John 4:4 says:

> *"You are of God, little children, and have overcome them, because He who is in you is greater than he who is in the world."*

We need to possess this knowledge, this truth. We need to enforce it by God's wisdom and grace to see our mountains fall.

I visited the online edition of Webster's 1828 dictionary and looked up the definitions of both own and possess. They are as follows:

Own: 1. "To have the legal or rightful title to; to have the exclusive right of possession and use. A free holder in the United States owns his farm. Men often own land or goods which are not in their possession."

Possess: 1. "To have the just and legal title, ownership or property of a thing; town; to hold the title of, as the rightful proprietor, or to hold both the title and the thing. A man may possess the farm which he cultivates, or he may possess an estate in a foreign country, not in his own occupation. He may possess many farms which are occupied by tenants. In this as in other cases, the original sense of the word is enlarged, the holding or tenure being applied to the title or right, as well as to the thing itself."

We may own promises of the Lord that we still may have to contend for to possess, agonizethe over. Think of the Promised Land. That inheritance was Israel's. It was a promise God had given them. It was theirs, yet they did not yet possess it until they went in and conquered.

Most likely, our conquering will not be easy. Your enemy does not want to give up the territory of your life that he has stolen. But you are the sole owner of your inheritance in Christ so do not be robbed. Go after that Promised Land and lay hold of it in Jesus name.

Open The Door Of Faith

I have a tendency to put God in a box. I also have a tendency toward black and white thinking. The latter is not too terrible, especially in the kingdom of God where all truth resides. But being too stubborn in either direction in today's mental health awareness climate, black and white thinking will get you a diagnosis of mild Asperger's Syndrome. One of the symptoms is the inability to see or understand and/or incorporate anyone else's point of reference or view.

And so it is sometimes in my struggle with a particular situation, I see it one dimension in this time frame. My Father in heaven however, sees the situation in multifaceted dimensions in the light of eternity.

Sometimes the answer we are searching for is so easy. It can be right in front of us and still we miss it. I use the example for people who smoke and want to quit. The answer is easy, quit smoking. Easy answer, right? It's walking through it that's the hard part.

Mid-way into my decision regarding leaving for school, the Lord gave me such an easy answer with all the clarity that was needed to understand it.

About a month or so earlier I wanted to have an adventure

with my sister's two youngest children. We talked about it and decided that we were going to go off into the unknown and do some hiking. I picked them up the morning of our trip all ready to go. After saying good-byes we headed from my sister's house to my car. I got in the driver's seat and watched as my nephew opened the front door to get in. I told him that he couldn't sit up front because of his age and the air bags, and that he needed to sit in the back seat. He looked puzzled and said that he knew, as he searched up and down the side of the front seat. He asked how he was going to get back there. I told him, just open the door.

He was used to two door cars with front seats that lift forward allowing him to gain entrance to the back seat. My car was a four-door car, which he had totally missed when he came up on it. He had missed that there was an alternate method or way of entering.

God reminded me of this story one morning in prayer when I was crying out to Him for an answer of what to do. He said just open the door. How simple His answer, how profound was His meaning.

Christ was telling me to open the door of faith, go through and trust Him for the outcome. Like the time at the oceanfront with my children and the storm approaching. He would be faithful to guide my inner man and lead me where He wants me to be.

I used the excuse for all of my mental turmoil during this difficult decision making period that the problem was not with Christ's directive, but with myself, thinking that I hadn't heard correctly, doubting what I was hearing, fearful of making a mistake and stepping out of God's will. What it actually comes down to is trusting God.

> *"For you have formed my inward parts; you covered me in my mother's womb." Psalm 139:13*

He knows our frame and our purpose, and He will be faithful to fulfill our destinies if we allow Him.

Our greatest purpose is to represent Him and take dominion as He has ordained it. Genesis 1:26 says:

> *"Then God said, Let us make man in Our image, according to Our likeness; let them have dominion over the fish of the sea, over the birds of the air, and over the cattle, over all the earth and over every creeping thing that creeps on the earth."*

In each sphere that God places us, we are to represent Him, take dominion by the power and authority He has given us, and so bring Him glory. On that note, no matter where we are, if we are faithful to take dominion for Christ, there will be no area that will be a total mistake or failure. Taking dominion has to be done in Christ, therein is the great qualifier. It must be an act of obedience and love for our Father and by His great power, not our own selfish will or desires.

Continued Communion
With The Father

"Behold, I stand at the door and knock. If anyone hears My voice and opens the door, I will come in to him and dine with him, and he with me."

Revelation 3:20

The opening of the door in the previous entry is not entirely different then the message Christ speaks in the above passage. Here Jesus is talking to the Lukewarm Church, a complacent church. The note in my study bible says individuals may still open the door and enjoy intimate fellowship with the Lord, that He wants for the door to be opened shows the paradox of grace and personal responsibility.

The scripture reference to standing at the door is Song of Solomon 5:2.

"I sleep, but my heart is awake; it is the voice of my beloved! He knocks, saying, "Open for me, my sister, my love, my dove, my perfect one; for my head is covered with dew, my locks with the drops of the night."

The rest of the passage in this chapter of the Song is not one of pleasantness and joy, but a melancholy ache because of her disobedience. Verse 5 said she took off her robe and washed her feet- her own act of independence making her ill prepared and unpresentable for her beloved. She then takes matters further into her own hands and goes looking for him, only to be mistaken for a harlot and stricken by the watchman.

Reading this passage gave me holy fright at the thought of my doing something that would turn my beloved Jesus, away. It is in these moments of weakness that the enemy tries to beat me down and tell me I blew it and that I missed the turn miles back.

What keeps me going is God's grace and His love and the truth of His Word that condemns those lying voices. The danger is there for anyone to fall into passivity. We must waken full force and guard against it.

Matthew Henry expounds on this passage in this manner:

1. "The indisposition that the spouse was under, and the listlessness that seized her (verse 2): Here is 1. Corruption appearing in the actions of it: 1. Sleep. The wise virgin slumbered. She was on her bed, but now she sleeps. Spiritual distempers, if not striven against at first, are apt to grow upon us and to get ground. She slept, that is, pious affections cooled, she neglected her duty and grew remiss in it. She indulged herself in her ease, was secure and off her watch."

2. "Grace remaining, notwithstanding, in the habit of it: "My heart wakes; my own conscience reproaches me for it, and ceases not to raise me out of my sluggishness. The spirit is willing, and after the inner man, I delight in the law of God, and with my mind I serve that. I

am, for the present, overpowered by temptation, but all does not go one way in me. I sleep, but it is not a dead sleep; I strive against it; it is not a sound sleep; I cannot be easy under this disposition.""

Note (1) "We ought to take notice of our own spiritual slumbers and distempers, and to reflect upon it with sorrow and shame that we have fallen asleep when Christ has been nigh in His garden."

(2) "When we are lamenting what is amiss in us, we must not overlook the good that is wrought in us and preserved alive: "My heart wakes in Christ, who is dear to me as my own heart, and is my life; when I sleep, He neither slumbers nor sleeps."

"Christ knocks to awaken us to come and let him in. He knocks by His Word and His Spirit. He knocks by afflictions and by our own consciences...He calls sinners into covenant with Him and saints into communion with Him. Those whom He loves, He will not let alone in their carelessness, but will find some way or other to awaken them...When we are unmindful of Christ He thinks of us, and provides that our faith fails not."

It is God at work in us both to will and do His good pleasure, but we have to be fully aware of the prowling lion seeking whom he can devour.

1 Peter 5:8:

> *"Be sober, be vigilant; because your adversary the devil walks about like a roaring lion, seeking whom he may devour."*

Satan lives and longs to consume our holiness and passion. We have to guard against this daily.

Christ so lovingly calls His beloved using such terms of endearments as: my sister, my love, my dove, my undefiled. These are the whispers of my Master's voice when I am feeling unloved that I need to listen for. He assuredly does call to us in this manner. He doesn't unbraid us in our mistakes and human frailties, but contrarily, woos us back unto Him. What love! What grace!

Is the door of your heart open to God's calling of sanctification and grace? There are many Christians out there that don't believe in sanctification, of walking in true holiness, playing the grace card that God accepts them just the way they are.

Christ is still knocking. He knocks to gain entrance and if we are remiss, we will not hear Him knocking for us to commune with Him. Be prepared. Be presentable. Answer the call. God is calling us unto himself.

The satisfaction in self is a sign of complacency. The satisfaction in Christ is a sign of wholeness.

Wouldn't you rather be wholly resigned to be truly satisfied in the depth and richness of Christ?

Conversation In Heaven

Our conversation is in heaven. Or at least it should be. I need to remind myself of this on a daily basis. When I'm trying to figure out life and the messages of men, God calls me to talk with him and keep my conversation vertical.

This morning in prayer I thought of drawing a straight, vertical line on a card. It will be a reminder to me that my relationship with my Father should be a vertical one. I need to remember that all my conversations need to be pointed upward. I also need a representation reminding me that no space exists between us. This leaves me no room to look elsewhere for answers.

I just (only after 1/2 of a century) learned that when I bring a situation to my father first instead of anyone else, the situation resolves much more quickly.

If I tell my father my complaints, issues, and heartaches rather than running to a close confident in hopes of commiseration, He works on my heart so quickly, the emotional charge or sting that I felt to match whatever situation it was that I was dealing with, dissipates almost immediately.

When I don't turn the situation to Him immediately, the wheels of my mind churn incessantly. I try and figure out what this or that person said or meant by what they said; what their actions or lack thereof meant; thinking, analyzing, contemplating the hurt, the injustice, the miscommunication.

This of course does absolutely no good. What it does do is keep me in a constant state of annoyance, anxiety, and/or apprehension.

David penned in the Psalms not to fret, that it only causes harm. It is that spiritual mindset that my father wants me to be at constant work at. Will I be attuned to the spirit, or attending to the temporal? The spirit is willing but the flesh is weak.

Since we are spiritual beings, and need to be spiritually minded, it only follows that we need to bring our prayers silently to Christ. This is where the war is waged, and that being said, nothing that we say or do physically can add one iota to our stature.

1 Peter 2:23 gives us an example of Jesus' silence and His conversation being only with His Father:

> *"Who, when He was reviled, did not revile in return; when He suffered, He did not threaten, but committed Himself to Him who judges righteously."*

It's very difficult when someone reviles us not to react, or at the very least to get a word in edge wise.

This verse references Isaiah 53:7:

> *"He was oppressed and He was afflicted, yet He opened not His mouth; He was led as a lamb to the slaughter, and as a sheep before it's shearer is silent, so He opened not His mouth."*

Perhaps our Father referring to us as sheep is not a bad thing after all. (I say this tongue in cheek, of course). Jesus gave us the perfect example of what our response should be as His righteous followers.

Have you ever been in a conversation with someone and as the words are coming out of your mouth you are thinking I shouldn't be saying this? Complaints about another person or situation, gossip cloaked as a prayer request, justification of your own actions? The list of verbal misconduct is endless and James tells us that *the tongue is a fire, a world of iniquity.* (James 3 - for further instruction and admonition read the whole chapter!)

God exhorts us in 1 Peter 3:8

> *"Finally, all of you be of one mind, having compassion for one another; love as brothers, be tenderhearted, be courteous;*
>
> *Not returning evil for evil or reviling for reviling, but on the contrary blessing, knowing that you were called to this, that you may inherit a blessing.*
>
> *For He who would love life and see good days, let him refrain his tongue from evil, and his lips from speaking deceit.*
>
> *Let him turn away from evil and do good; let him seek peace and pursue it.*
>
> *For the eyes of the LORD are on the righteous, and His ears are open to their prayers; but the face of the LORD is against those who do evil."*

Ahh, it's that turn the other cheek again. No, it's more than that. It's the attitude of the Spirit. There is not a thing that we can do on our own without God's help and grace. If He has seen that the vessel He is molding in us needs this particular instance to deal with and be given the opportunity to make the correct choice, He will insure that we have everything we need unto grace and godliness. We only turn to the world because we want constant validation and acceptance. God gives us so much more.

Again God exhorts us in Philippians 2:14 & 15:

> *"Do all things without complaining and disputing,*
>
> *That you may become blameless and harmless, children of God without fault in the midst of a crooked and perverse generation, among whom you shine as lights in the world."*

These are great words with a promise of a blessing attached to them if we are successful. We are on a glory walk toward perfection. Of course we will never, ever attain it in this life. If we ever feel like we "have arrived", we'll need to check our pulse. The only time that we are going to arrive at fully comprehending God's perfect will and fully grasping all the characteristics of God, we will be beyond the pearly gates, not down here chatting with our neighbor.

Read the words again. The promise is that we may become blameless and harmless, without fault in the middle of this mess! In awe I read about Jesus' comment when He saw Nathaniel coming toward Him in John 1:47:

> *"Behold, an Israelite indeed, in whom is no guile." (KJV)*

Would that be Jesus' response if He saw us walking toward Him today? I would love it if that were His response when He saw me walking toward Him, but I fear it would not be.

Do a self-check today and be honest with yourself about where you bring your complaints. Who do you talk to when life throws continuous curve balls your way and the injustices keep mounting. When you are frightened and feel like the odds are stacked against you, do you go to a quiet place and tell your Father? I would encourage you to begin the habit - try this for a day, a week, a month, until it becomes a habit. That you will not complain, you will not gossip, you will not seek out like-minded sympathizers. Instead go into your prayer closet and share your heart with your Father.

I guarantee that an audience with God will do better than what previous audiences have done for you. He is not just an ear to hear, He is the great fixer and mender of all people, hearts, attitudes, unfair situations, and the endless myriad of the host of evils that beset us.

That means in addition to getting a listening ear, you will get the peace that passes all understanding in your heart and grace to walk out the rest of your issue. His Word promises it and His Word is true.

The Economy Of Heaven

While we are on the subject of heavenly things, I wanted to share a story about what I feel is a good depiction of what God's economy is all about and how I came to terms with the idea that God holds my purse strings.

I have a great-niece who is six years old and who single handedly made my birthday an event I will probably never forget because of her generosity.

Before my move out of state, I was living with my sister. She and her family wanted to celebrate my birthday and so planned a casual get together in our back yard. As they prepared to come over for the party, my niece's second youngest daughter became very concerned regarding my gift. My niece, who is an unemployed single mother of six children, barely making ends meet, had nothing to give. Grace, who is used to certain traditions that my niece has instigated with her children, naturally assumed they would carry over to me since I am part of her extended family.

Each year the children in her family receive birthday presents, but they also get a dollar bill for each year, adding up to whatever year they are celebrating. (Remember, this is my 50th! Whoo Hoo!!) With this in mind Grace asks her mom what they are giving me. Her mom answers that she couldn't afford a gift.

Grace was adamant that I needed a gift and so went off to find a treasure.

She didn't settle for any old thing, she gave me her best. It was a vibrant turquoise wrap with seahorses and sea animals splattered all over it in the brightest colors imaginable. My niece said that it was her favorite. She used it daily, dressing up in it, making a tent between the couches with it, using it as a doll blanket and sleeping with it. Nobody in the family could believe that Grace would even think to give it away, much less part with it.

Once she had wrapped it up all by herself, she asked her mom where my birthday card was. Again, her mom reiterated that as much as she would like to have purchased one for me, she just didn't have the extra couple of dollars. With that answer my niece told me that Grace cried MOM! Aunt Hannah NEEDS a birthday card, and set off to make me one.

Then, the two final questions came. How old was I turning and where was the money that they were going to put into the card? (Who is this kid??) Her mom patiently explained the lack of ability for their family to provide this last part of the gift as well. Grace then quietly set off to find her own purse and with the last $1.26 that she had in her wallet, proceeded to stuff my envelope with it. She didn't give me some of what she had left from her precious savings; she gave me all of it.

I opened her envelope with the beautifully decorated birthday notes and the $1.26 not knowing any of this. After my niece filled me in on the details I went to Grace and told her that her mom said she had given me her absolutely favorite scarf. She looked at me and replied matter-of-factly, "that's right, it was, and now I want you to have it."

I relate that story because it is the single, most generous

encounter I have ever experienced and because I believe it captures the essence of how God wants us to view our wealth, whether it is $1.26 or a million dollars. The world's system of money connected to greed, lust, and covetousness is contrary to the economy of heaven. At the heart of Heaven's economy is a Father's promise that He will provide all of our need according to His riches in glory.

Hebrews 13:5&6 speaks to that:

> *"Let your conduct be without covetousness; be content with such things as you have, for He himself has said, I will never leave you nor forsake you.*
>
> *So we may boldly say: The Lord is my helper; I will not fear, what can man do to me?"*

The note in my study bible regarding this passage says that "covetousness and financial fear are overcome by a contentment founded on the assurance of God's constant presence and the promises He extends to us to supply our daily needs. Because of the word of assurance that He Himself has spoken, we may boldly respond with a declaration of confidence."

When I start to get uptight about money I just reassure myself of God's promises and tell Him of my need. He is incredibly quick to meet my need. It is not always exactly how I anticipate it will be met, or at the exact moment that the need occurs, but usually the outpouring is better than I hoped and more creatively produced.

The more that we keep our mind stayed on God and His precepts and take hold of His promises of provision, the world's system loses its controlling influence over us. If, through no fault of my own, I cannot make ends meet - there have been instances of forced unemployment, injuries leaving me incapable of working full time, etc... then the Lord has promised to be my provider. I will lay hold of the promises in His Word. Like King Hezekiah who laid his complaint out before the Lord in 2 Kings 19:14, I will lay my complaint out and ask for the Lord to help.

In the above reference, Sennacherib was threatening King Hezekiah. Instead of reacting to the physical realm, Hezekiah receives the threatening letter, reads it and then goes up to the house of the LORD where he proceeds to spread the letter out before God and then prays a prayer of faith.

That biblical example needs to be our stance.

During times of financial need, people have come forward with money and other necessities. I have been given automobiles multiple times, and from various people over the years, when I have had transportation issues. When the Lord provided me with a house, people gave me furniture, and the list throughout my life goes on and on. Provisions of health, sound mind, healthy bones, wisdom, and favor are also some of God's provision that we don't typically think of, but are foundational aspects of our spiritual economic system.

When you are worrying about your finances, ask God for forgiveness in the areas that you have not been a good steward and then do what Psalm 55:22 tells us:

> *"Cast your burden upon the Lord and He shall sustain you. He shall never permit the righteous to be moved."*

The word sustain in this passage is Chul, Strong's #3557 and means "to maintain, nourish, provide food, bear, hold up, protect, support, defend; to supply the means necessary for living,"

God will not let his people starve or die. Psalm 37: 25 & 26 says:

> *"I have been young, and now am old; yet I have not seen the righteous forsaken, nor his descendants begging bread.*
>
> *He is ever merciful, and lends; and his descendants are blessed."*

You may experience hunger, but it will not be the end of you. I had a year of my life where my income did not match my budget. Not only did I not have any wiggle room, no matter how hard I tried to make ends meet, the needs to income ratio just did not match up. Often times I was hungry and often times afterward I asked the Lord why He allowed that lengthy season.

His answer was that He wanted my sufficiency to be in Him and to learn to hunger and thirst for righteousness over daily food. I also think He used food as a lesson because this has been a previous area of weakness in my life, where I had used food to fill a void that only God could fill.

When we truly get our priorities straight with God regarding provision and finances, it is one of the most freeing and liberating experiences. When you trust God for your supply and not complain against providence, you will be amazed at what He will show you and how He will enable you to gather and reap.

I am not talking about prosperity theology, God as puppet provider. I am talking about a God who sees a real need in one of His trusting children and makes a way where there seems to be no way. Who sustains (Chul) when we abide in Him and trust Him to sustain us. Then covetousness, greed, and ties to that which does not ultimately satisfy will fall away. And then, like my niece Grace, giving away a prized possession for the pure joy of making someone else's special day monumental will become second nature.

Think you can do it? For the pure joy set before you give up something you treasure for someone else?

Swimming Against The Stream

A few years ago, I had been working at a job that I loved. My employment was in the area that I went to grad school for, and one that had always been the desire of my heart - to work with children.

It was a long time coming. I had done my internship within this realm, but after grad school the job opportunities were not as ripe as I had first anticipated, and so when I landed this job, although it was not at the clinical level that I had hoped, I was grateful for the opportunity and loved the kids that I worked with.

Have you ever worked in a sphere where as a follower of Jesus you swam against the stream? God's Word is full of exhortations to us to be in the world but not to touch it; to expect trials; warnings that the world is at enmity with Christ; reminders telling us that we don't belong here, and that this world is not our home. We should expect that we will encounter situations where we will be swimming against the stream and it will be tough!

In Isaiah 59:15 he says: *"...and he who departs from evil makes himself a prey."*

Matthew Henry's commentary says about this verse "They treat him as an enemy who will not partake with them in their wickedness. He that departs from evil is accounted mad; so the margin reads. Sober singularity is branded as folly, and he is thought next door to a madman who swims against the stream that runs so strongly."

I'll suffice to say I was swimming against a very strong current and although I was considered a "good clinician with great skills," I was not considered a "team player" and the latter won out in the long run.

For weeks I cried out to the LORD as to what to do all the while trying to discern His answer regarding my quest for moving away to go to Bible school. It was difficult, to say the least, to walk into an atmosphere of tension and disdain on a daily basis.

Then the transmission in my car went for the second time. The first time was two years earlier when my daughter owned it. Now, under my ownership its breakdown couldn't have come at a worst time (or so it seemed).

One of the stipulations of the job was the requirement to have reliable transportation. Almost all of my clients lived at least 30 minutes away and with some of them I had to drive additional distances to group activities or for recreation.

Through various conversations that I had with my boss during our weekly supervision meetings my last month there, I discerned she was giving me the opportunity to bow out gracefully from my employment. However, I felt the Lord was telling me to hang in there, that is, until the final morning I was to meet with my boss for supervision.

I was sitting at my desk praying prior to our meeting. I felt impressed that the Lord was telling me that this day was His timing for me to quit. As a middle aged, single woman with no job prospects on the horizon I can't tell you the vexation I felt at previous times, thinking about this possible outcome. But this morning I had total peace that God was in control and this was the thing to do.

I went in and told my boss that I had enjoyed working there and was glad for the opportunity that she had given me. But that I felt she was giving me the opportunity to bow out gracefully and quit. As I spoke of resigning she nodded her head in agreement. When I got done talking she said good, and that she wouldn't have to give the termination letter that was in her hand.

I felt both saddened and relieved at the same time and although I did not have a fall back plan, source of income, or job leads lined up, the incredible feeling of liberation pervaded all of my senses. I felt that how the scenario had played out was totally God's doing.

I had worried about the requirement of reliable transportation when I had first gotten the job, because I was having problems with mine at the time. God got me through to the exact moment that I needed it.

I don't know what was wrought in the spirit during that season. I do know that I prayed fervently for my work sphere every day. I prayed for my fellow workers, for my clients, for their families, and for all of the people involved in care taking of the children that I worked with. I believe to this day there was a reason for it, and my prayer is that someday the Lord will give me a glimpse as to what it was. If nothing else it could have been for the furtherance of my spiritual development and that in itself was a great gain.

I still had so many questions for God. Here I was out of work and again leaning hard into my Father to help me stand.

We were created to worship God. We are commanded to take dominion. It is through Christ's power and by His grace only that we can do this, because when you stand for the kingdom of God, saint, you are waging war with enemy strongholds.

After I left work that day God led me to scriptures in Isaiah to encourage me and help me understand the meaning of being a child of God in a hostile environment and bearing his light in a dark world.

One of the passages is in chapter 9, which talks about the increase of the Lord's government. The other speaks to how the entrance of Christ's government brings light to those who sit in darkness. Isaiah 61:1-4

> *"The spirit of the Lord God is upon me, because the LORD has anointed Me to preach good tidings to the poor; He has sent Me to heal the broken hearted, to proclaim liberty to the captives, and the opening of the prison to those who are bound;*
>
> *To proclaim the acceptable year of the LORD, and the day of vengeance of our God; to comfort all who mourn;*
>
> *To console those who mourn in Zion, to give them beauty for ashes, the oil of joy for mourning, the garment of praise for the spirit of heaviness; that they may be called trees of righteousness, the planting of the LORD, that He may be glorified.*
>
> *And they shall rebuild the old ruins, they shall raise up the former desolations, and they shall repair the ruined cities, the desolation of many generations."*

We minister Jesus giving of a cool drink of water to a parched soul in the work place. It's a smile or a word of acknowledgment to someone who feels invisible. It is validation to a child that has been fed messages of worthlessness. It is the invisible realm of the Spirit where God works supernaturally and where, although we may never see nor understand, our prayers ARE effective.

The Lord was showing me this and encouraging me that He always makes a difference when He shows up, if we are faithful to be His witness, silently through prayer, or vocally through evangelism. Most importantly though, it is our actions that people will notice.

Is there a person, a family member, loved one, or situation that you feel called to be committed to interceding for? Just remember that all things are possible for Christ. Be faithful to stand where your Father has placed you for however long the season is that you are there, and pray. But pray expectantly! Pray believing that God wants to give you and/or, them the victory and then watch the walls crumble and the victory enter!

Remember that it is not about you and me and what our personal level of comfort is. God is more concerned that we intercede in His name, represent Him, and stand in faith in the sphere that He has placed us, then whether or not we feel we fit in and are one of the "team".

We are totally accepted in the Beloved and that's what really matters because that is where our self-worth stems from, Christ.

Don't acquiesce to the world's systems around you for the sake of ease. But, do be wise as a serpent and gentle as a dove, operating in God's wisdom for His namesake. Through all the challenges, never, ever deny Him and He will never deny you.

Faith's Enemy, Doubt, & The OK's That Are Not

"Now the serpent was more cunning than any beast of the field which the LORD God had made. And he said to the woman, "Has God indeed said, 'You shall not eat of every tree of the garden'?"" Genesis 3:1

It is important to keep your eyes focused on the vision that God has given you, your mind centered on Christ, and your heart devoted to His purpose. It is within a short time that the enemy can come in and try to unbridle your relationship with Christ. The first thing that happens is he begins to plant seeds of doubt in your mind.

He will try to tell you that this is all there is. You may experience feelings of diminished self-worth and loathing trying to enter and lie against the fact that you are a child of the Most High King. That fact alone measures out a godly inheritance, and strength like no other. You see, God's kingdom turns the world's understanding upside down, for when we are weak, God is strong and His purposes cannot be thwarted.

Next the enemy of your soul might try and show you all the reasons not to trust. Maybe you don't have a car, making travel inconvenient or impossible; perhaps you don't have a mate and wonder if the Lord understands your heart's desire, or maybe that He has forgotten you; perhaps you saw yourself in a different position and wonder if your purpose will be fulfilled. It only takes one bad circumstance and a negative reel spinning in our head to let doubt creep in.

What about your heart? Are you sold out for Christ? Truly sold out so that nothing else matters and in fact pales in comparison to Him? Are you spending time in His presence? Lavishing Him with praise and thanksgiving? Have you been taking time to tell Him how much you love Him, and do you study to show yourself approved?

These are difficult questions that we need to ask ourselves so that we don't fall from grace. We can play the grace card all we want, but at the end of the day has God won out over our slothfulness, laziness, procrastination, preoccupation, or a jammed schedule?

I read a blog about a book review the other night in which the author spoke about a particular book he had liked well enough, but recommended another book over it. He felt that the author of the first book had not spoken out about what our responsibility was in a particular realm of Christendom, thus bearing a very lopsided view of our walk with Christ.

I appreciated the author's point of view. I believe that there are many conditions regarding obtaining God's blessings that have the propensity to be overlooked. We have an important and grave responsibility to represent Christ with love and honor in holiness. Yes, as humans we are prone to sin, but thankfully we have a forgiving God. This does not give us license to live unholy lives.

Wake up saint! Years ago the new age dawned and placated

Christians with the OK's. It's OK to...and you fill in the blank. Smoke? It's a drug and powerful escapism tool. God's Word tells us not to give our minds over to anything but the Holy Spirit. Not to mention the adverse effects that smoking has on your body which as 1 Corinthians 6:19 & 20 tells us:

> *"Or do you not know that your body is the temple of the Holy Spirit who is in you, whom you have from God, and you are not our own?*
>
> *For you were bought at a price; therefore glorify God in your body and in your spirit, which are God's."*

How about the OK to NOT read God's word daily? He knows your schedule and how difficult it is for you to fit in time for that. What? I had a friend who used to say that we have it backward in the kingdom of God. We think we are too busy to pray or spend time with the Lord. In all actuality, doing just that increases our time because the Lord can give us increase in both productivity and mental focus.

It is very difficult to follow God's way and to keep our mind focused on His Word if we haven't gotten daily doses of it. We can't give a word in season if we haven't been in the Word and prepared for the situation that God sees is coming our way.

That's how lovingly the Holy Spirit leads. To give you the word prior to whatever circumstances you encounter, (already pre-ordained by Christ) arming you with the word necessary for yourself, or making you ready to minister to someone who needs that balm.

What about it's OK to skip praying, or that because we are so busy we can pray in the bathroom, or driving in the car, or while we are busy with our daily tasks? God tells us to pray without ceasing in 1 Thessalonians. That means never stop praying never. So yes, pray in all of those places, but also heed God's Word and go quietly into your prayer closet and pray. Pray kneeling and be reverent to our Holy God because He is worthy. He hears the prayer of the needy, and James 5:16 says:

> *"Confess your trespasses to one another, and pray for one another, that you may be healed. The effective, fervent prayer of a righteous man avails much."*

What about the-it's OK not to love? I went through a period of my adult Christian years not liking people. I felt perfectly justified because I couldn't stand what I was seeing. I also felt much more comfortable being alone than around people, so the cycle I found myself in self-perpetuated. Then one day the Lord laid on me 1 John 4:20 & 21.

> *"If someone says, "I love God," and hates his brother, he is a liar; for he who does not love his brother whom he has seen, how can he love God whom he has not seen?*
>
> *And this commandment we have from Him: he who loves God must love his brother also."*

It could not have been clearer to me. God was telling me to love those that I had kept at arm's length. It was Christ that enabled me to do this. Looking back on the years then, compared to how I feel about humankind now is amazing to me. As God moved on my heart I was able to give people the benefit of the doubt and God increased my heart further by letting His love flow through me.

Remember, as Christians we are to show Christ's love to a dying world. If we don't, there is no one else who will. His love is what it's all about. Don't just extend it and then be done if it's not reciprocated. In a lot circumstances it won't be. The enemy's grip on the minds and hearts of people is strong. He will make them think you have an ulterior motive, or some kind of conspiracy. Just be genuine and continue to ask God for grace. God will give it if we remember that it's not about us, it's about the other person and the only person we need to think about pleasing is God. This is a sobering thought.

I may be preaching to the choir here. I know that I write for myself to stay in constant reminder. I fear that as a fallible Christian I am guilty of all of the aforementioned things.

Back to my earlier mention of the blogger - how do we do it? How do we discipline ourselves into holiness? How do we love genuinely with Christ's love? How do we wake up day after mundane day and receive strength and the grace that we need? By asking Christ to fill us and believe that He will.

Pray believing that our Christian walk is not about what we do, but what Christ does through us.

I can't tell you the number of times I have been at my morning job, dreading my afternoon job and have cried out to the Lord for strength and grace and He has met me in incredible ways. So much so that by the end of the day I am in awe that I didn't just survive, I thrived! Hopefully I did everything to the glory of the one who made me.

God is not a respecter of persons. If God helps me to overcome, He will help you too.

The "it's OKS to" has a host of other items that we have become numb to and Satan has tried to use as a measure to begin to build a wall of blindness to our spiritual state. His goal is ultimately to get us so far removed from what God intended in our relationship with Him that when we arrive in heaven on that day, God will say I knew you not.

Revisit the previous entry's scripture verse in the 61st chapter of Isaiah and reread verse 4. Commit to be a repairer of any broken areas in yours or your family's lives and let the Lord use you to be instrumental in rebuilding those ruins.

In His Hands

"My sheep hear my voice, and I know them, and they follow me.

And I give them eternal life, and they shall never perish; neither shall anyone snatch them out of my hand.

My Father, who has given them to Me, is greater than all; and no one is able to snatch them out of My Father's hand.

I am my Father are one." John 10:27-30

I read an article entitled "Brandwashing and Biblewashing" [8] in the February 2012 edition of *Table Talk* magazine. The author was Dr. David Murray, professor of Old Testament and Practical Theology at Puritan Reformed Theological Seminary in Grand Rapids, Michigan.

What caught my attention was his reference to a grocery store in close proximity to my home, Whole Food store. In the article Dr. Murray told about their marketing schemes to get shoppers in a certain mind mode for buying. What was attention grabbing to me however was his example of the capacity for both the subconscious and conscious mind to be brainwashed by the evil one on a daily basis. I know and believe this and have wrestled with this issue on a number of occasions.

Dr. Murray cites a story about the illusionist Derren Brown, and his experiment to prove how susceptible we are to the thousands of signals we are exposed to each day. He invited two advertising, what the author termed "creatives", to visit his office to discuss some marketing ideas. On the way to his office brown arranged clues to appear surreptitiously on posters, balloons, window shops, and pedestrian t-shirts.

When the two showed up, they were given 20 minutes to come up with a campaign for a fictional store. At the end of the allotted time, the two placed the ideas they had come up with in a sealed envelope and submitted them to Brown. Brown opened them up to find that the plans for the campaign were similar to his own design with a 95% overlap. Dr. Murray's summation on that scenario was if Derren Brown could do that to advertisers; think what the devil can do to you.

Then there's GOD. That's what I have to keep reminding myself. I am well aware of the devil's schemes and attempts of seduction that he places on my life. Daily I pray for the mind of Christ, protection with Christ's armor, spiritual weaponry for casting down arguments and pretensions that exalt themselves against God. And still I tremble.

I fear. I began to write that I don't, but truth be told, I do. I know the Lord gave me the verse that I am about to share with you and that story so that He could do a work in my mind (and heart), that would teach me not to fear no matter what the enemy tries to throw at me.

"Yes, He loves the people; All His saints are in Your hand..." Deuteronomy 33:3

In regard to this passage, Matthew Henry says "the shepherd is so careful of their (His saints) welfare that He has them not only within His fold, and under His eye, but in His hand." (Remember back how we are engraved in our Father's hand?).

His note goes on to say: "The saints are preserved in Christ Jesus and their salvation is not in their own keeping, but in the keeping of a Mediator. The Pharisees and rulers did all they could to frighten the disciples of Christ from following him, reproving and threatening them, but Christ saith that they shall not prevail...His Father is greater than all...He is greater than all the combined force of hell and earth. He is greater in wisdom than the old serpent, though noted for subtlety; greater in strength than the great red dragon, though his name be legion, and his title principalities and powers. The devil and his angels have had many a push, many a pluck for the mastery, but have never yet prevailed."

Revelation 12:7 & 8:

> *"And war broke out in heaven: Michael and his angels fought with the dragon; and the dragon and his angels fought,*
>
> *But they did not prevail, nor was a place found for them in heaven any longer."*

I believe in, and personally have experienced the Almighty's power. I have experienced it many times, so my fear is not of what man can do to me. It is not a frightful fear; it is a holy fear that causes me to be ever watchful, ever vigilant because our enemy prowls about seeking whom he can devour and I don't want it to be me.

I am so thankful that because God says His Word will not come back void. In my weak states of vulnerability, I can pray to His own Word back to Him – 1 John 5:18-20:

> *"We know that whoever is born of God does not sin; but he who has been born of God keeps himself, and the wicked one does not touch him.*
>
> *And we know that we are of God, and the whole world lies under the sway of the wicked one.*
>
> *And we know that the Son of God has come and has given us an understanding, that we may know Him who is true, and we are in Him who is true, in His Son Jesus Christ. This is the true God and eternal life. "*

When I pray His Word I can feel His strength lifting me up and into a crisp clarity in my mind that even at my age when I begin to forget the little things, I can remain confident of whose mind I have.

One of my favorite books of all times is Max Lucado's Cosmic Christmas. [9] Each year at Christmas time I would haul out my decorations and books and that was one of the stories my son and I would read chapters of each night before bed.

Max recounts the story of Jesus' birth, beginning in the throne room with an assignment to Michael to carry the vile containing God's precious seed to be given to Mary. The enemy is present and tries then, and at many times throughout the story to oppose and prevent the angel's mission of both the vile from arriving to earth, and to stop the birth from taking place, through a variety of wicked schemes and subtleties.

Each time, although there are some close calls where the lead angel almost falls for a few of the enemies guises, the angels begin to praise and pray, thereby thwarting the plan of the enemy instead of the other way around. There is nothing like praise and worship to confound wicked spirits.

I have thought about that story many, many times over the years. I realize when I praise and pray, the draw of the world, the lies, and crafty cunning of the enemy fall away. Sometimes I have to do this numerous times. To my own dismay, although I'd like to say throughout the day, often it is a minute-by-minute exercise in having to take my thoughts captive in Jesus name.

The fight is worth it though because it is not only my future at stake, my eternal life is at stake. I would like to see the next generation and maybe even the one following it born into a Godly lineage, also unto eternal life. So I fight for them as well, the unborn ones whose destinies God has already planned.

It's nice to know that we have a mediator that has gone before us and that we are preserved in Christ Jesus. It is also nice to know that our salvation is not in our own keeping, but in the keeping of a Christ. No one can ever take us from His keeping.

Of Mop Handles
And Poppy Fields

I will lift up my eyes to the hills – from whence comes my help?

My help comes from the LORD, who made heaven and earth.

Psalm 121: 1 & 2

God knows the simplicity of my heart and so gave me a spiritual lesson the other day in a very tangible and physical manner. Since I love to ride my bicycle, God used this venue to speak to me.

Since taking our thoughts captive and daily putting on the mind of Christ, as well as the renewing our minds, are of the utmost importance, it stands to reason that our thoughts can be our own worst enemy.

I have been blessed this season with borrowing a bicycle for transportation. I purchased a bike trailer to go along with it, enabling me to haul the cargo that I need for my job and get where I need to be. I try to be thankful and cultivate an attitude of gratefulness, because it is hard work setting up and tearing down this gear multiple times a day. The Lord's grace prevails for me on most days. It's in the example that I'm about to share that enables me to consider it precious that the Lord knows just what I need to drive an important message home. (No pun intended)

I set out for my afternoon job on the bike. On this particular day I was trailer-less. The house I was going to clean had some of the equipment that I needed, thus enabling me to just ride equipped with just a rack bag without the extra burden of the trailer weight.

Google maps encouraged me that it was only about 12 miles away and so I felt confident that I would arrive at my destination within about 45-50 minutes.

It was a chilly day and I had a few extra moments so I decided as I left the office that morning, to ride home and get an extra jacket for warmth. I had eaten a good lunch and just happened to grab a candy bar when I was home, giving me a supreme edge on my energy.

I was all prayed up, thus grace was at an all time high, having previously asked the Lord for His benefits to be sufficient for the day.

Although the initial ride was ok, I felt a bit sluggish. My progress was at a much slower than usual pace. About half of the way there I felt like Dorothy in the Wizard of Oz walking through the poppy field. My sciatic nerve began to throb, my legs were tired, and although I was listening to worship music, my mind began to drift to thoughts of calling off and returning home.

When I was, what I thought to be only a few miles away, I called the office asking them to inform the customer that I would be about ten minutes late. Those ten minutes turned into about thirty. When I arrived I prayed for more grace to then get me through a three hour cleaning job, followed by the return bike trip home.

The job went fine and I set back out to return home. This time it was worse than before. I couldn't get the bike to move out of first gear, even though the terrain wasn't that hilly. The rack bag was about 40 pounds or so, but I didn't think that it was heavy enough to slow me down so much. After a few miles I pulled over to check and see if the brakes were sticking. They had done that before, making riding difficult.

I tried everything I knew to adjust the back brakes and still the wheel was not spinning. I began taking the gear off of my bike to take a closer look, enabling me to work on the bike a bit more unhindered. As I did I realized the problem.

The mop handle that I had bungeed to the back rack had slipped in such a way that it was stuck between the rack and the tire, making it impossible for the wheel to turn freely. I undid the bungee cords, reconfigured my gear, and then rode with such ease I couldn't believe the difference. Everything was fine. I was making up for lost time, riding hard and fast until about half way home I hit a sewer grate and popped the back tire. Hmpff.

When I had approached the intersection, instead of riding my bicycle in back of traffic I rode around the cars on the right hand side and hit the grate full force.

The flat tire incident turned out fine. I called my daughter and got a ride home and was no worse the wear for it. Just to digress for a moment, I feel when something like that happens, when God's provident hand steers our course in another direction than then one we set off on, that it is because He has a purpose in it. Perhaps He is keeping me from danger or He was helping me to appreciate the fact that I have someone to call. There was that, and He showed me that He had a lesson in all this as well.

I was tired, really, really tired. I could not remember the last time I had taken a bicycle ride and felt that way. I once took a 5-hour bike ride with my brother and that tired me out. But typically I have more than enough energy for such a short ride. I also woke up sore the next day, not having taken the adequate time to stretch my muscles, which I had stressed to the max.

As I thought back to the difficulty of the ride, inwardly I was a bit amused at my ignorance. It was my own fault that I had so much difficulty. I was also a bit embarrassed that the whole thing could have been avoided had I been more careful at the onset. Or...and here's a brainstorm of an idea - I could've stopped immediately to check out what the problem was instead of trying to push myself to extremes on a vehicle that was not working.

What I was impressed with from the Lord was that this scenario was analogous to taking thoughts captive. As I have mentioned before, sometimes it is a moment- by-moment action. One run away thought can set on course a whole series of events that are detrimental for our spiritual, and sometimes physical lives.

When our thoughts are not on God, but are centered on man or situations, or when we are focused on ourselves or on the negativity, we get bogged down like we're walking through the poppy field. Lethargy, depression, and melancholy, to name a few, can be signs of spiritual cause and effect of not having a Christ centered devotion. (Not to negate that Christians suffer from mental health problems - that is not the point).

When I am facing a challenge and begin to focus on the enormity of it instead of Christ's power, His power is not released through me to work in the situation. Then, instead of walking in His strength, I am bending under the weight of the burden.

Conversely, when my gear is properly packed and mounted and I am looking to Christ to be my all and all, I not only have His strength, but additionally His grace. No having to bend under the burden of Satan's harassments, I am journeying easily.

We need to be careful, very careful at every turn asking the Spirit not only for guidance, but to keep us in check for humility and purity. It's easy to be aware that I have a forty-pound pack on a bicycle not meant for sporting gear like that, and still not care about hitting an open metal grate due to impatience.

Similarly with our thoughts, we can be aware of what we need and should be doing for sanctification - knowing that the enemy prowls about like a roaring lion seeking to devour who he can, and still make the mistake of falling down in sin, or bottoming out with pride.

We need Christ every minute, every breath, every thought. Be armed, be ready, and be aware of the right focus and God will be protector, defender, shield, and guide.

The Just Shall Live By His Faith

I will stand my watch and set myself on the rampart, and watch to see what He will say to me, and what I will answer when I am corrected.

Then the LORD answered me and said: "Write the vision and make it plain on tablets, that he may run who reads it.

For the vision is yet for an appointed time; but at the end it will speak, and it will not lie. Though it tarries, wait for it; because it will surely come. It will not tarry.

Behold the proud, His soul is not upright in him; but the just shall live by his faith." Habakkuk 2:1-4

I felt inspired the other night to write again about faith. Faith is one of those gifts that God gives that you just can't say enough about. I had great ideas too. Unfortunately I got side tracked and didn't take the God given opportunity that I had, and as the way of some ideas go, forgot exactly what I was going to write about.

Still, I carried the thought regarding faith around with me for days. I then asked the Lord to give me the ability to release what message He wanted me to convey, and was impressed with the verse, "the just shall live by his faith."

What came to mind immediately with that impression were two questions - who are the just? And, what does it mean to live by his faith, especially with a tarrying vision?

The NKJ study bible I reference throughout this book has what's called a "Word Wealth" that gives a definition to select words. The word just was notated to a word definition for righteous at Lamentations 1:18. Strong's definition of the word righteous (#6662) "as tsaddiq. One who is right, just, clear, clean, righteous; a person who is characterized by fairness, integrity, and justice in his dealings. Tsaddiq is derived from the verb tsadaq, "to be righteous, justified, clear." Tsadaq and its derivatives convey justice and integrity in one's lifestyle. Being righteous brings a person light and gladness...It is the tsaddiq who shall live by his faith in Habakkuk 2:4."

John 3:36 also cited for Habakkuk 2:4 says:

> *"He who believes in the Son has everlasting life; and he who does not believe the Son shall not see life, but the wrath of God abides on him."*

We are made righteous (just) when we believe in the Son, Jesus Christ. Everlasting life is given to us and we belong to Christ, made clean by the spilled blood of the lamb. We have life in Christ because of our faith in Him.

So we see that we are made clean because of salvation, but we also walk in righteousness as tsaddiq also refers to a person who is characterized by fairness, integrity, and justice. Those are the just. We are the just if we know and believe on Jesus Christ and have a right relationship with him.

Romans 1:17 says:

> *"For in it the righteousness of God is revealed from faith to
> faith; as it is written, "The just shall live by faith.""*

And what does living by his faith mean? According to "shall
live" (Chayah) Strong's #2421 as cited in the Word Wealth in
the study Bible, it means "to live, to stay alive, be preserved; to
flourish, to enjoy life; to live in happiness; to breathe, be alive,
be animated, recover health, live continuously. The fundamental
idea is "to live and breathe." Breathing being the evidence of
life in the Hebrew concept...The present reference is one of the
giant pillars of the faith...it literally reads: "The righteous person
in (or by) his faithfulness (firmness, consistency, belief, faith,
steadfastness) shall live!"

As I contemplated the verse again I was awed by the fact that
it's all we have, our faith in Christ. But, it's not only all we
need, it far exceeds, above and beyond our wildest expectation,
the ability to live a life of wholeness, peace, joy, and prosperity
because of our fountainhead (God) in which our faith stands.

In the preceding chapter of Habakkuk the prophet looks around,
sees that evil men control the justice system, are overturning
righteous decisions and are mistreating the weak and the
helpless among them. Habakkuk is looking to the LORD for
help, asking Him a series of questions regarding His allowance
of such perversity. And then he waits for God's answer. He
waits patiently and he waits expectantly. He also waits with
humility, mentioning his contemplation of how he will answer
when corrected.

God does speak to him and tells him to hold the vision, for it
is yet to come. It is going to be a while and although it appears

as if it tarries - God's timing is perfect and it will come at the appointed time.

Matthew Henry's Commentary says of this verse "This vision, the accomplishment of which is so long waited for, will be such an exercise of faith and patience as will try and discover men what they are... Those who are truly good, and whose hearts are upright with God, will value the promise, and venture their all upon it; and, in confidence of the truth of it, will keep close to God and duty in the most difficult and trying times, and will then live comfortably in communion with God, dependence on him, and expectation of him. The just shall live by faith; during the captivity good people shall support themselves, and live comfortably, by faith in these precious promises, while the performance of them is deferred.

The just shall live by his faith, by that faith which he acts upon the Word of God."...

What vision has the LORD written on the tablet of your heart? Is it tarrying? Are you waiting for it? What does your faith stance look like?

I pray that the challenge that you face in believing the LORD for His implementation of your vision, proves your faith steadfast, and your strength firm. I pray that God's grace would enable you to wait patiently, with hope, and joy knowing that it will come not a moment too soon or too late. God will do it, rest in that. Live by your faith.

My Birthday Present

"The LORD reigns; let the earth rejoice; let the multitude of isles be glad!

Clouds and darkness surround Him; righteousness and justice are the foundation of His throne.

A fire goes before Him and burns up His enemies round about.

His lightnings light up the world; the earth sees and trembles.

The mountains melt like wax at the presence of the LORD, at the presence of the LORD of the whole earth.

The heavens declare His righteousness, and all the peoples see His glory."

Psalm 97:1-6

I saw the Lord's glory in a tangible manner the eve of my 50th birthday. I'll be selfish for a moment and say that I believe it was my Father's birthday gift to me. He knew that since I was unemployed I did not have any money for celebration, so He provided it to me free of charge. And since it was at night and I was in bed without my glasses, He made sure that it was larger than life so that I wouldn't miss a thing. It was spectacular!

I had gone to bed that evening and instead of laying in my usual manner on my bed, decided to take the fan out of my window and lay in the opposite direction, with my head at the foot of my bed by the window. It had been a warm day and there was a nice cool breeze coming in, making it for perfect sleeping weather. Wanting to take full advantage, I positioned myself accordingly.

It was the middle of the night when I awoke out of a sound sleep. The sky was fairly light for that time of night, colored with a pretty pinkish-orange hue. I looked out of my window to the west and saw that lightening was striking and I had a perfect view of it. It was like watching a fourth of July fireworks finale for over an hour. My expression is just too limited to put into words the beauty of that event. I will suffice to say that it was by far the most incredible light show I had ever seen. No thunder, a beautiful sky, and huge, bright, white bolts of light in the sky directly in my line of view.

As I lay there watching, in awe and appreciating the solitude of the moment, I was incredibly aware of God's presence and power. He would use this display to speak to me later in the day to say that He, who suspends the clouds in the sky, holds me and mine. To tap into this reality is powerful!

God's Word in Psalm 19:1-4 states:

> *"The heavens declare the glory of God; and the firmament shows His handiwork.*
>
> *Day unto day utters speech, and night unto night reveals knowledge.*

> There is no speech nor language where their voice is not
> heard.

> Their line has gone out through all the earth. "

We know that God reveals Himself to us through His Word
and through nature. That night, God's revelation to me through
nature couldn't have been clearer. That He wanted me to witness
it was also evident to me that I woke up without provocation and
was able to watch without being too lethargic to stay awake.

The next day I had the pleasure of spending the day with my
son. It was my choice on what I wanted to do, so I chose one
of my favorite past-times, hiking. I have a couple of spots in
Ithaca that I love so we spent the day there, hiking and enjoying
the waterfalls of Buttermilk Park, and then shopping at the
Commons in Ithaca. Because at that time my son was living
on the East coast, I didn't get the opportunity to see him that
often, so spending the day with him was another special God-
ordained gift for me.

As all moms care about the health and safety of their children,
I do as well, and am doubly concerned for their spiritual state.
Until God reveals Himself personally to anyone, we are in a state
of blindness. Since there are spiritual land mines and fowler's
snares everywhere in our world, this can be a cause of great
consternation for parents regarding their unsaved children.

During spending time with my son, the Lord reminded me
about the astounding natural display of the night before. He
encouraged me of His power, and reminded me that the One
who suspends the heavens, will watch over and care for my
children.

Take this to heart if you are a parent praying for the salvation of your children. God, who breathed life into existence, who spoke and the world was, who gives the oceans their boundaries, and suspends the stars and the clouds in the sky, is the same God who holds you and yours.

Position yourself in a manner that will be most effective in your prayers, asking the Holy Spirit to give you the battle strategies, and faith to see your prayers through. Believe in a Heavenly Father who delights to give his kids good things - hearts desires, birthday gifts, protection, and love. And watch for the creative ways that God answers prayer and fulfills our need for reassurances along the way.

Our Shield Is Christ

"After these things the word of the LORD came to Abram in a vision, saying, "Do not be afraid Abram. I am your shield, your exceedingly great reward." Genesis 15:1

The Lord gave me this scripture some time ago, which I have quoted back to Him on numerous occasions, asking Him to be my shield as He was to Abram.

I want to unpack this in a moment, but first interject this thought. I smiled to myself as I began to write this entry at the thought of Abram being afraid. I didn't smile in a mocking sense, like ah hah Abram, man of God, is fearful. But that the Lord had to calm the fears and encourage the men of great renown, just like He comforts me.

Another example that I have visited from time to time is in the first chapter of Joshua. God says to Joshua, "Be strong and of good courage" four times. Joshua was one of the spies who came back unmoved by what his eyes had seen when they were sent out to survey the Promised Land. Going forward the Lord knew that for such a duty that Joshua was undertaking (carrying Moses' mantle) that Joshua would need some encouragement.

These examples help me not to feel so bad when I experience the need for my Father's reassurances. To know that if indeed the men of incredible faith such as Abraham and Joshua needed God's comfort and support periodically, how much more then would the Father understand a weak woman such as myself might need some extra care too.

At this particular juncture of his life, Abram needs God closer than ever before. Matthew Henry says of this verse that, "where there is great faith, yet there be many fears", and references 2 Corinthians 7:5 where Paul says:

> *"For indeed, when we came to Macedonia, our bodies had no rest, but we were troubled on every side, outside were conflicts, inside were fears."*

Paul also understood the dichotomy of walking in great faith yet experiencing anxiety.

I have the tendency to be harsh with myself and to treat a mistake as failure. I tend to be too analytical (usually on the wrong things). And I also view my personal weaknesses and misgivings as character flaws, causing me to feel that God must somehow get exasperated with me. So when I see that comrade in arms were also challenged on like front in their faith, I feel comforted that maybe God really understands my human frailty. (Of course He does).

The other reason this verse brings a smile to my face is God says He is *our* exceedingly great reward. Like we deserve anything but death, and here in His infinite mercy and grace, He tells us, He is our great reward! Oh how *"The lines have fallen to me in pleasant places; yes, I have a good inheritance!" Psalm 16:6*

How awesome God is to choose us and give us such a gift! Such a reward as Himself! That all being said, the real reason that I wanted to reference this verse was in regard to the shield.

Hannah Rose

We are called every day to put on our armor of Christ and be battle ready. There are some days when we will be tried more in a defensive manner. Then there will other days when we need to be ready on the offensive. In all actuality we need to maintain readiness on either side.

The shield that we are to pick up is to deflect the fiery darts of the wicked one. It's our shield of faith, enabling us to speak faith into a particular circumstance, gaining our composure and strength in Christ to go on. Our shield enables us to discern the lies and tactics of our adversary and let Christ's Word and truth absorb them.

When God acts as our shield, He is able to cover our entire body. This is both in the spiritual realm and in the physical sense. I love the picture that Max Lucado paints for us in his book Cosmic Christmas, that I have previously mentioned "In His Hands" entry. This is a story of God sending down His angelic forces to deliver the vile containing His seed for Mary to conceive Jesus, and for the angelic host to protect her and insure that she is kept safe and that the babe is born.

In one particular scene Mary and Joseph are in a wagon on their way to Bethlehem when Satan's forces attack them. Mary tells Joseph that she is in terrible pain and that it is like something is hitting her in the stomach. The story reads that Gabriel wrapped himself around her like a shield and that the demons swords pierced him.

This is God as protector in such a tangible sense.

I believe that God will be to us what we believe Him to be. That if we have faith to move mountains, mountains will move. If we have faith to see our dead brought back to life, we are going to hold out for that miracle and see it happen. However, if you believe that God is this far off, ethereal creature uninvolved in the personal affairs of man; who made creation like a big clock, started it ticking and then left it alone, most likely He will be uninvolved in your life.

Matthew 13: 58 tells us that Jesus did not do many mighty works in His own country because of the people's unbelief. On the other hand if you believe that everything God's word says about Him is true, He will be all that and more. God works on the behalf of His own.

I love Mark 16:17 & 18, the promise of being kept from harm for those who steadfastly believe:

> *"And these signs will follow those who believe: in My name they will cast out demons; they will speak with new tongues;*
>
> *They will take up serpents; and if they drink anything deadly, it will by no means hurt them; they will lay hands on the sick, and they will recover."*

No harm will come to Christ's own when they purpose to believe God's miraculous power in a situation ordained by Him.

Psalm 91:9-12 is a striking illustration of God's divine protection for those who dwell in Him. It fully encompasses the safety of abiding in Christ.

> *"Because thou hast made the LORD, which is my refuge, even the most High, thy habitation;*
>
> *There shall no evil befall thee, neither shall any plague come nigh thy dwelling.*

> *For He shall give his angels charge over thee, to keep thee in all thy ways.*
>
> *They shall bear thee up in their hands, lest thou dash thy foot against a stone."*

That's where Gabriel comes in as mentioned in our story, wrapping himself around Mary. God gives His angels charge over us.

Put on your armor of Christ today and every day. Pick up that shield of faith and quench the fiery darts of the wicked one. Remember to ask Christ to be your shield as He was for Abram.

If you happen to experience a day where you feel weary or weak, know that as you call upon God, He will be to you a warrior, outfitted for battle against your enemies, and will protect you from harm.

The Beauty Of God's Presence

"The LORD you God in your midst, the Mighty One, will save; He will rejoice over you with gladness, He will quiet you with His love, He will rejoice over you with singing."
Zephaniah 3:17

I encourage you to take some time and sit in your Father's presence. Ask Him for an encouraging word, one of love and affirmation. He will send it. He knows that you need to hear how much He loves you. Remember, He is your shield, your exceedingly great reward. Marvel at the thought of that for a while.

I have already mentioned that I struggle with negative voices. So I need a good dose of my Father's love frequently. I remind Him that He promises to be a husbandman to me, in addition to being my Father. In turn, He reminds me that He never forgets.

Zephaniah 3:17 is one of my all-time favorite verses. To think of God rejoicing over me! The reference given for rejoices is Isaiah 64:5 and the Word Wealth in my study bible indicates Strong's #7797 "Sus: To rejoice, be glad, be greatly happy. Sus is one of the Hebrew words for "rejoice."... From this verb is derived Sason, a noun meaning "joy, rejoicing, gladness." Sason is quite evident in Esther 8:16; Psalm 45:7; Isaiah 12:3; 61:3; and Jeremiah 31:13.

These verses describe a rejoicing that is the complete antithesis of mourning; it is a pervasive, irresistible joy. That blows my mind.

Think about the connotation of that definition in regards to the Zephaniah 3:17 verse for a moment. Imagine God rejoicing over us with gladness, being greatly happy with a pervasive, irresistible joy! I'm sorry, maybe it's those negative voices again, but on my best day I can't imagine I am that pleasing to the Lord.

But I am, and you are too. God's word tells us so and God's word does not lie.

The second reference made to this verse is to Habakkuk 3:18:

> *"Yet I will rejoice in the LORD, I will joy in the God of my salvation."*

The word for joy is also referenced in the Word Wealth to Strong's #1523 "Gil: To joy, rejoice, be glad, be joyful. Gil contains the suggestion of "dancing for joy," or "leaping for joy," since the verb originally meant, "to spin around with intense motion. This lays to rest the notion that the biblical concept of joy is only "a quiet, inner sense of well-being." God dances for joy over Jerusalem and because of His people. (Isaiah 65:19 and Zephaniah 3:17)."

We have a father who delights in His children. His word tells us in Jeremiah 31:3

> *"The LORD has appeared of old to me, saying: "yes, I have*

*loved you with an everlasting love; therefore with loving
kindness I have drawn you.""*

I went through a season where the LORD opened my ears to the
women around me and I realized that right within the church
walls were some of the most needful, insecure souls.

In trying to be an encourager, I would remind them of what the
salvation status means. It means that if God is a King, we are
the daughters of the Most High King. Come on, it doesn't get
any better than that. Having a king for a father!

Years ago on one very rainy, bleak, and dark day back in my
hometown, my interior frame of mind matched the weather.
Very thinly I began to crawl out of the darkness I was in and
went to run some errands. As I drove along on my way to the
grocery store, I began to pray. It was one of those days we all
have now and then, sure that people are looking at you with
something negative on their minds. (As if we, God's children
should care), unfortunately, sometimes we do. It's that old need
of wanting to feel accepted.

As I exited my car and went to the service desk to take care of my
business, the stares and glares loomed from the passer-bys and
I was feeling a bit more insecure. I began to encourage myself
saying that it didn't matter whatever people were thinking of
me, God loves me, He is my Dad AND He's King! I'm the
daughter of the Most High King!

That was my mantra in and out of the store that day. Did I
mention it was raining? How about windy? When I got back
into the car I realized that the stares that I had gotten were
not imagined, they were real. I wear my hair with bangs across
my forehead and usually give them a good douse of hair spray
to stay in place. That day was not an exception and due to the

weather, my bangs probably had more than the usual dose. As I had walked through the wind and the rain into the store, the wind had caught my bangs and swept them up. Because of the hairspray, they nicely stayed in place - sticking straight up from my forehead. (Got to love those old school aerosol sprays!)

No wonder people were looking. They were probably wondering how (and why) anyone in the world gets their hair like that. I had a great laugh in spite of myself.

That's what we have to do. We have got to be easy on ourselves on the days when we need to be and remember who we are in Christ. We need to let the joy that He dances over us with illuminate the sphere around us so that we will be ready to give an answer for the hope that is in us as 1 Peter 3:15 tells us:

> *"But sanctify the Lord God in your hearts, and always be ready to give a defense to everyone who asks you a reason for the hope that is in you, with meekness and fear."*

Nothing can separate us from the love of our father, according to Romans 8:38 & 39 tells us:

> *"For I am persuaded that neither death nor life, nor angels nor principalities, nor powers, nor things present nor things to come,*

> *Nor height nor depth, nor any other created thing, shall be able to separate us from the love of God which is in Christ Jesus our Lord."*

Isn't it comforting and good to know in a fallen world where people will fail you; loved ones will come up short; friends sometimes will not stand the test of time; even some of you will experience your own children turning their back on you and/or God, that Christ will never fail you?

Get in His presence. Lavish Him with love, but remember we have nothing of our own to give Him, it's all in Him and by Him that we live and move and have our being. As you honor your father, accept His love. He wants to pour over you and have you understand the depth of His unconditional love for you today and every day.

I leave you with this parting scripture passage out of Ephesians 3:14-19:

> *"For this reason I bow my knees to the Father of our Lord Jesus Christ,*
>
> *From whom the whole family in heaven and earth is named,*
>
> *That He would grant you, according to the riches of His glory, to be strengthened with might through His Spirit in the inner man,*
>
> *That Christ may dwell in your hearts through faith; that you, being rooted and grounded in love,*
>
> *May be able to comprehend with all the saints what is the width and length and depth and height –*
>
> *To know the love of Christ which passes knowledge; that you may be filled with all the fullness of God.*

Accept that prayer and the Father's love today.

Grumbling, Mumbling, Grudging, And Complaining

"Speaking to one another in psalms and hymns and spiritual songs, singing and making melody in your heart to the Lord,

Giving thanks always for all things to God the Father in the name of our Lord Jesus Christ." Ephesians 5:19 & 20

Are you a complainer? Take a moment now and ask yourself and be honest. Do you give thanks to God in ALL things? Do you glorify your God for His providence no matter what your circumstances?

Verse 20 takes a minute to chew and digest, doesn't it? Giving thanks ALWAYS for ALL things to God the Father in the name of our Lord Jesus Christ. I don't know about you but I am not seeing, nor hearing any exceptions in those verses. We are called to be encouragers, filled with thanksgiving.

You might already be visiting that issue in your life. Perhaps God has already shined His spotlight on this area and wants you to have success in overcoming with your mouth. Or maybe you are like most of us and you are saying, no, not me. The majority of us do not even need to ask if this is a problem area for us, we already know in our heart what's the matter with our mouth and attitude.

Personally, I love a great sympathizer. One who will hear my problems, commiserate with me, and let me feel that I am justified in voicing my complaints. Do you know what God says about our complaining? Philippians 2:14 says:

> *"Do ALL* (emphasis mine) *things without complaining and disputing."*

Side reference defines complaining as grumbling, and for disputing, it is arguing. (NKJ).

Here is the KJV translation:

> *"Do all things without murmurings and disputings."*

This verse references 1 Peter 4:9 which says:

> *"Use hospitality one to another without grudging."*

OK, that pretty much covers it. Combine the above scripture verses and you have: no grumbling, mumbling, complaining, murmuring, grudging, disputing, arguing, or any verb with the ing suffix that you can think of. Why? Because when you complain you give your negative words power and they take flight and gain momentum.

Proverbs 18:21 "Death and life are in the power of the tongue, and those who love it will eat its fruit."

With our words we bring life, or with our words we add to the weariness and emptiness of life.

God wants *"That you may become blameless and harmless, children of God without fault in the midst of a crooked and perverse generation, among whom you shine as lights in the world."* Philippians' 2:15

This is the verse following how to do all things. Giving us reason for righteous behavior for our God who wants us to shine for Him with no dimmer switch on!!

Remember today, no complaining.

Grace Land

I told you in the beginning of the book that I would come back to my mention of the Paul Simon song, Graceland. As I near the finish of this compilation I wanted to do just that.

A friend of mine once asked if I had ever experienced De'-Ja' Vu. The "been there, done that" experience you have when you are at a place for the first time. Or the feeling comes over you that you have already done the exact thing you are currently doing, even though you've never done it before. Although I don't agree with the label, admittedly I have had those moments.

My reply to her, and my most humblest of ideas on the matter is in reference to Psalm 139, especially verse 16 which says:

> *"Your eyes saw my substance, being yet unformed. And in Your book they all were written, the days fashioned for me, when as yet there were none of them."*

I believe (and again, I stress that this is my humble opinion), that like we, and all of our days, like our very complex DNA code, are written by God's own hand contained within a package. Without getting too metaphysical here, we know that we are both spiritual creatures and physical ones. We, the package, have been already written by God the Author, who knows everything there is to know about us, every hair, every idea, every choice, every circumstance, every outcome, all of it.

God is on an eternal continuum that we can't begin to touch. I believe that He touches other dimensions that we can't begin to tap into. The exception for us I think, are those rare moments where things seem hauntingly familiar like you have experienced them before.

Could it be God's Spirit in us witnessing God's eternal unexplainable sequence already, like DNA coded into us?

So here it is, I'm in Florida with absolutely, and I mean absolutely no thought of going Tennessee, and inwardly I begin to sing the lyrics, "we're going to Graceland, Graceland, Memphis, TN"... in my head. And, it's exactly where I ended up.

Peculiar to me as well, in August in one of my journal entries I wrote that I had been anxious and unable to sleep, uneasy at the thought of going to Florida? No, I wrote Tennessee. At that moment I also had absolutely no idea or desire to go to Memphis and yet here I erroneously wrote the wrong state for my destination. It was obviously not the wrong state according to God's design.

It wasn't exactly a De´-Ja´ Vu experience; some psychologists might call it some type of Freudian slip. I prefer to think of it in view of Psalm 139:16:

> *"...and in Your book they all were written, the days fashioned for me, when as yet there were none of them."*

It wasn't a De´-Ja´ Vu thing, the Eternal was touching the finite and I was getting a glimpse, even unknowingly of what was to come.

Memphis is where I am now, by the very circuitous route from Rochester to Orlando Florida first. It is all, I believe, God ordained. I have to believe that, otherwise I would not be here. God has a purpose for me here, not yet completely unfolded.

I had lived here in 2008 and returned to New York to finish school. Except for my daughter, I had no other ties here and no thoughts of ever returning.

My heart-rending disappointment occurred in the summer of 2011 when my daughter later told me she was marrying a Memphian. I love her choice, a young man, recently saved. Her decision should have made me delighted.

But I knew that meant that she would want to stay there with him in Tennessee and put her roots down, not return to her home state of New York. Knowing that I had no desire or forethought to ever return to Memphis, I was gravely disappointed. Little did I know that is exactly where God would lead and have me return to.

I am excited to see all that God has for me here, in His grace land.

Hope Deferred

"Hope deferred makes the heart sick, but when the desire comes, it is a tree of life."

Proverbs 13:12

If someone asked you to draw a picture of longing, what would it look like? Personally I can hardly draw stick figures, much less a picture worthy of meaning. When I was in kindergarten I came home crying one time because we had an arts and craft project to draw a fish. We were supposed to draw the fish, color both sides and then cut it out. The idea was that when they were finished, the teacher was going to punch a hole in the top, tie string to them and then suspend them from our kindergarten room ceiling.

Only, I couldn't draw so I sat there terrified at the prospect of even trying. I have to say that as I recall, the teacher wasn't all that compassionate with me. I do remember however that she gave me two huge pieces of that murky tan construction paper; you know the kind that actually still had the pulp of the trees in it and was longer than your desk was wide? During free time the next day, when all of the other children would be playing, I was to continue to try to create this fish. I am sure that the extra piece of paper was given in great faith that I would make a mistake and need another piece.

I came home that day defeated. I burst through the door of my house and spilled my woes to my mom. She was more compassionate than the teacher and encouraged me to take my time, offered me some suggestions of how to get started, and prayed.

I don't remember any more of that story. I don't remember finishing the fish. I don't remember the teacher's reaction to it when I did. And I don't remember staring at it proudly as it swam above me in my schoolroom. But I remember now what it looked like, because my mom saved that fish, all those years.

You have to understand something about my mother. She survived the depression and so was a bit (understatement) of a pack rat. She didn't however save many things from our childhood. Possibly because she had 8 children and anything surviving childhood would have been a miracle.

She gave it back to me one day in a paperback New Testament. She had carefully wrapped it Cling Wrap and tucked it into the book. Her message to me was something like she knew all things were possible with Christ. At the time she believed God for my salvation.

She lived to see that prayer answered. Her dead was brought back to life.

That's a lengthy story to tell you that I can't draw, but if I *could* draw, my picture of longing would be a vast and dry desert. It's the very color of the construction paper that my kindergarten teacher gave me, and as long. I know I just opted for an easy way out of drawing a picture, because what does a desert look like for the most part, except creamy brown colored desolation? Picture a void that cannot be filled.

I love the scripture that I opened with because it is packed with an intensity of hope beyond my wildest dream. I have what I consider promises that the LORD had spoken to me through His Word and prophets that I am still waiting to come into fruition. It has been a long, long, long, long, long time. Can I say LONG time? And I'm still waiting.

There have been times that I have been heartsick over what I wait for. I have felt the void of the loneliness the longing has created. I have sat in the desolation of the wait.

Because the Lord has made a promise to me I know without question that when my desire is realized it will be a tree of life. It will be God's life filling up all the voids that this life has created in me.

About a half a dozen years ago I felt impressed that the Lord said hold tenaciously to that promise and do not let go, because there will be some seasons of your life where it will look impossible to fulfill, or it will look as if I have forgotten you and this will not be so. I was so glad for that message because exactly what my Father said would happen, has. I have had moments where what I am waiting for has looked completely and irrevocably impossible.

Not for God.

This was the last time that my heavenly father and I communicated about it. Sure I still offer up the to the Lord petitions, pleas, complaints, prayers, moanings, and questions. I ask the father if he has forgotten me. I remind Him that I am a vapor quickly fading. (Although in actuality what I really mean is I am quickly drooping, sagging, wrinkling, balding...) He knows. He knows and so He does not negate my supplications and He gives ear to my nonsense babblings, but He also knows that His promise is tucked in my heart and it cannot be moved.

I love Hannah's song of the Old Testament. She had her tree of life realized. 1 Samuel 2:1-10:

> *"And Hannah prayed and said: my heart rejoices in the LORD; my horn is exalted in the LORD. I smile at my enemies, because I rejoice in Your salvation.*
>
> *No one is holy like the LORD, for there is none besides You, nor is there any rock like our God.*
>
> *Talk no more so very proudly; let no arrogance come from your mouth, for the LORD is the God of knowledge; and by Him actions are weighed.*
>
> *The bows of the mighty men are broken, and those who stumbled are girded with strength. Those who were full have hired themselves out for bread, and the hungry have ceased to hunger. Even the barren has borne seven. And she who has many children has become feeble.*
>
> *The LORD kills and makes alive; He brings down to the grave and brings up.*
>
> *The LORD makes poor and makes rich; He brings low and lifts up.*
>
> *He raises the poor from the dust and lifts the beggar from the ash heap, to set them among princes and make them inherit the throne of glory. For the pillars of the earth are the LORD's, and He has set the world upon them.*
>
> *He will guard the feet of His saints, but the wicked shall be silent in darkness. For by strength no man shall prevail.*
>
> *The adversaries of the LORD shall be broken in pieces;*

> *from heaven He will thunder against them. The LORD*
> *will judge the ends of the earth. He will give strength to*
> *His king, and exalt the horn of His anointed."*

This has spoken to me time and time again, knowing that the Lord's power can do for us what we think is impossible. He takes the barrenness of this life and fills it with His essence, birthing His plan, providing hope and a future.

I look toward the future for the fulfillment of my tree of life. Can you imagine the scene? The Lord knows what we wait for and when it's His will and perfect timing the desire will be realized. It will be a tree of life to him who waits for it.

Because it's something that I do so often it seems, (wait) I looked up the word waits in Strong's and found two different meanings:

"Wait: Qavah: Strong's # 6960. To wait for, look for, expect, hope. Qavah is the root of the noun tiqvah, "hope" or "expectancy." Qavah expresses the idea of "waiting hopefully".

Also - "Yachal: Strong's #3176: To wait, tarry, hope, trust, expect; be patient; remain in anticipation. Yachal is often translated "hope"."

The correct way to hope and wait for the Lord is to steadfastly expect His mercy, His salvation, and His rescue, and while waiting, not take matters into one's own hand.

This is a difficult task to be sure, to not take matters into our own hands. I think for the strong-willed people (like me), God gives situations that are impossible to take into our hands so that when fruition of time finally comes there will be absolutely no doubt in anyone's mind that the Lord did this. That He answered the prayer.

These are also faith building and character forming times. It is not easy to wait for something, much less waiting hopefully, expectantly, patiently, and with trust. No nervousness that God has forgotten you. No anxiety that you are waiting in vain. No judging God's ways. No trying to make it happen any sooner than God's appointed time.

Just wait for that wonderful tree of life.

I forgot to mention early on that the only thing I feel I am capable of drawing with any talent (and remember I can barely draw stick figures) is a tree.

When I would sit down and color with the children in my life, I would inevitably end up drawing the same picture. I draw a tree with lots of branches, surrounded by green grass, flowers, and birds flying in the sky. (It's easy to draw flying birds - you just have to draw elongated m's. As far as the flowers go, if you are painting, you can just paint a green line for a stem and then smoosh your paint brush into the paper with the color flower you desire). (Intro to Drawing by Hannah Rose)

That will be Christ's masterpiece painted in my life, *my* tree of life. When it is realized I have a feeling it will be more magnificent than any tree I could ever imagine drawing.

Imagine that hope deferred in your life and how God will answer it. Dream of it. Pray for it. Then wait to see how and when God answers it. Know that you are not waiting in vain, but wait with joy and you will not be robbed of the richness and the incredible joy that you will experience in your journey during your wait.

The Song Of Moses

In the book of Deuteronomy, chapter 32, it is recorded that the Lord God speaks to Moses and tells him that the day is approaching when he will die, and asks him to call Joshua so that he may inaugurate him.

The Lord warns Moses that the people will turn their back on Him and break their covenant with Him. So God asks Moses to write down a song to teach to the children of Israel. The purpose was to bring continually to mind to the people of Israel the covenant God made with them.

I love it because I often forget from day to day and week to week the lessons that God had taught me through my trials. Sometimes in the mundane and ordinary of day-to-day life, I lose the beauty of God's lessons and the place of passion that my heart once held regarding these lessons. I need a constant reminder. The other thing I love about it is that God is referred to the Rock. The underlying note in my Bible terms this title as the essence of stability and reliability.

My ending prayer for you as you read this beautiful and poetic song is that you would remember that our God is a rock – He is The Rock. He is dependable, faithful, loving, and nurturing. He wants only what is best for us all.

When we are faithless, He is faithful. When we forget, He reminds us. There are dangers lurking. Keep His covenant commands as you walk through the storms and stress, along with the beautiful and calm, and you will be held in a place of peace. Deuteronomy 32:1-43

"Give ear, O heavens, and I will speak; and hear, O earth, the words of my mouth.

Let my teaching drop as the rain, my speech distill as the dew, as raindrops on the tender herb, and as showers on the grass.

For I proclaim the name of the LORD: ascribe greatness to our God.

He is the Rock, His work is perfect; for all His ways are justice, A God of truth and without injustice; righteous and upright is He.

They have corrupted themselves; they are not His children, because of their blemish: a perverse and crooked generation.

Do you thus deal with the LORD, O foolish and unwise people? Is He not your Father, who bought you? Has He not made you and established you?

Remember the days of old, consider the years of many generations. Ask your father, and he will show you; your elders, and they will tell you:

When the Most High divided their inheritance to the nations, when He separated the sons of Adam, He set the boundaries of the peoples according to the number of the children of Israel.

For the LORD's portion is His people; Jacob is the place of His inheritance.

He found him in a desert land and in the wasteland, a howling wilderness; He encircled him, He instructed him, He kept him as the apple of His eye.

As an eagle stirs up its nest, hovers over its young, spreading out its wings, taking them up, carrying them on its wings,

So the LORD alone led him, and there was no foreign god with him.

He made him ride in the heights of the earth, that he might eat the produce of the fields; He made him draw honey from the rock, and oil from the flinty rock;

Curds from the cattle, and milk of the flock, with fat of lambs; and rams of the breed of Bashan, and goats. With the choicest wheat; and you drank wine, the blood of the grapes.

But Jeshurun grew fat and kicked; you grew fat, you grew thick, you are obese! Then he forsook God who made him, and scornfully esteemed the Rock of his salvation.

They provoked Him to jealousy with foreign gods; with abominations they provoked Him to anger.

They sacrificed to demons, not to God; to gods they did

not know, to new gods, new arrivals that your father did not fear.

Of the Rock who begot you, you are unmindful, and have forgotten the God who fathered you.

And when the LORD saw it, He spurned them, because of the provocation of His sons and His daughters.

And He said: 'I will hide My face from them, I will see what their end will be, for they are a perverse generation, children in whom is no faith.

They have provoked Me to jealousy by what is not God; they have moved Me to anger by their foolish idols. But I will provoke them to jealousy by those who are not a nation; I will move them to anger by a foolish nation.

For a fire is kindled in My anger, and shall burn to the lowest hell; it shall consume the earth with her increase, and set on fire the foundations of the mountains.

I will heap disasters on them; I will spend My arrows on them.

They shall be wasted with hunger, devoured by pestilence and bitter destruction; I will also send against them the teeth of beasts, with the poison of serpents of the dust.

The sword shall destroy outside; there shall be terror within for the young man and virgin, the nursing child with the man of gray hairs.

I would have said, "I will dash them in pieces, I will make the memory of them to cease from among men." Had I not feared the wrath of the enemy, lest their adversaries should misunderstand, lest they should say, "Our hand is high; and it is not the LORD who has done all this. " '

For they are a nation void of counsel, nor is there any understanding in them.

Oh, that they were wise, that they understood this, that they would consider their latter end!

How could one chase a thousand, and two put ten thousand to flight, unless their Rock had sold them, and the LORD had surrendered them?

For their rock is not like our Rock, even our enemies themselves being judges.

For their vine is of the vine of Sodom and of the fields of Gomorrah; their grapes are grapes of gall, their clusters are bitter.

Their wine is the poison of serpents, and the cruel venom of cobras.

'Is this not laid up in store with Me, sealed up among My treasures?

Vengeance is Mine, and recompense; their foot shall slip in due time; for the day of their calamity is at hand, and the things to come hasten upon them.'

For the LORD will judge His people and have compassion on His servants, when He sees that their power is gone, and there is no one remaining, bond or free.

He will say: "Where are their gods, the rock in which they sought refuge?

Who ate the fat of their sacrifices, and drank the wine of their drink offering? Let them rise and help you, and be your refuge.

'Now see that I, even I, am He, and there is no God besides Me; I kill and I make alive; I wound and I heal; nor is there any who can deliver from My hand.

For I raise My hand to heaven, and say, "As I live forever,

If I whet My glittering sword, and My hand takes hold on judgment, I will render vengeance to My enemies, and repay those who hate Me.

I will make My arrows drunk with blood, and My sword shall devour flesh, with the blood of the slain and the captives, from the heads of the leaders of the enemy." '

Rejoice, O Gentiles, with His people; for He will avenge the blood of His servants, and render vengeance to His adversaries; He will provide atonement for His land and His people."

If you have read that all in one sitting, I would encourage you to read it again and really meditate on all that is contained within.

I have a glimpse of understanding now at the seasons I have walked through, a culmination finally coming to head as I dig into God's word in this Song of Moses.

Hannah Rose

Verses 26-28 spoke to me through Matthew Henry's exposition on them:

> "After many terrible threatenings of deserved wrath and vengeance, we have here surprising intimations of mercy, undeserved mercy, which rejoices against judgment, and by which it appears that God has no pleasure in the death of sinners, but rather they should turn and live."

There is a person that I am close with and in regard to her walk with God think if only she did things thus and so, things would be much better off for her. Who am I to say? I have been in the same misguided place and even now have blind spots that only God can see and show me when He determines the proper time to work on that particular aspect of my character. (Lesson one million and...)

God has been merciful to me and brought me thus far in my life through every necessary trial, fire, and error, (because I am fallible, I'm sure there will be more to come), to bring me to a place of greater faith and trust, and life in His Spirit. Thus enabling me now to be able to look at a situation and know that God is in control; that I can trust Him for the outcome even though it might be serious or even dreaded.

I believe that is what God wanted for His people in the wilderness trials - their faith and trust and worshipful thanksgiving.

Have you asked God to show you your blind spots? Have you asked Him to give you an undivided heart? He will be faithful when we come humbly to Him, asking Him to show us, to mold us and make us aware, even in a greater way, of our need for our savior.

Going back to what I wrote earlier about Matthew Henrys writing that God has no pleasure in the death of sinners, but would rather they should turn and live, now gives me great hope for those whose lives I am believing God's salvation for.

Not by might, nor by power, but by thy Spirit, O LORD God Almighty! I think God allows us to a pinnacle of heights within and of ourselves before He mercifully acts, so that He can let us experience first-hand the meaningless of this life, of man's power, of the lies the enemy would have us believe of seduction, and money, lust, and knowledge. Then we learn the importance of following Christ wholeheartedly, and where our treasure should lie.

The last note in Matthew Henry's Commentary says: "Those may die with comfort and ease whenever God calls for them (notwithstanding the sins they remember against themselves) who have a believing prospect and a well-grounded hope of eternal life beyond death."

It seems to me to be the summation of all things. Until this world loses its grip on one's soul, we are not whole-heartedly serving Christ.

When all fades away and Christ becomes our hope and salvation, when we look more forward to eternity than being here on earth, we then own a piece of paradise in our souls. Fear loses its grip on us because then we can truly say, what can man do to me? The worst outcome is death, and if I were to die I would go home and be with my Maker. If any other situation befalls me it is that the glory of the Lord may be more apparent upon me (if I am faithful in the circumstance to walk with honor) and unto God.

Moses got to see his beloved Canaan from afar, but reconciled to his God now he would see a far more magnificent Canaan in eternity. I would love my promised land here and now, the desires of my heart realized and promises granted. But, if God has another idea for my life here on earth, I await my promised land in the hereafter.

References

1. The New Strong's Exhaustive Concordance of the Bible. James Strong, LL.D., S.T.D. Copyright 1995 Thomas Nelson Publishers

2. Webster's Online Dictionary. www.1828.mshaffer.com

3. Future Grace by John Piper. Published by Multnomah Publishers, Inc. and published in Britain by Inter-Varsity Press. Copyright 1995 by John Piper

4. Westminster's Confession of Faith Publisher Presbyterian and Reformed Publishing Company. Copyright 1964. ISBN 10 0875525385

5. The Holy Bible, New International Version. NIV Compact Thinline Bible. Copyright 2002 by The Zondervan Corporation

6. How the Gospel Brings Us All the Way Home by Derek W. H. Thomas. Copyright 2011. Published by Reformation Trust Publishing a division of Ligonier Ministries 400 Technology Park, Lake Mary, FL 32746

7. Intercessory Prayer by Dutch Sheets. Published by

Regal Books A Division of Gospel Light. Ventura, California, U.S.A. Copyright 1996 by Dutch Sheets

8. TableTalk Magazine published monthly by Ligonier Ministries, Inc., 421 Ligonier Court, Sanford, Fl 32771.

9. Cosmic Christmas by Max Lucado. Published by Word Publishing Nashville, Tennessee. Copyright 1997 by Max Lucado

About the Author

Hannah received a BA in Psychology and a MS in Counseling, but the greatest thing she has ever received is her gift of faith.

Through her faith, she provides encouragement and exhortations, using personal anecdotes and God's Word.

Hannah lives in upstate NY with extended family.